12 COMPELLING TRUTHS

Why Biblical Faith Is Completely Reasonable

Dewayne Bryant

© 2010 by Dewayne Bryant
2809 12th Ave S
Nashville, TN 37204
All rights reserved.

ISBN: 978-0-89098-477-2

Unless otherwise indicated, all Scripture quotations are from The Holy Bible, English Standard Version® (ESV®), copyright © 2001 by Crossway. Used by permission. All rights reserved.

Cover design by Jonathan Edelhuber

Dedication

To my beautiful wife Christa.

Introduction

Antony Flew shocked the world in 2004 when he announced that he had given up on atheism. His leanings toward Christianity had been rumored for several years, but he denied their validity. The announcement of his conversion to deism prompted a flurry of activity on the Internet. Christians heralded the conversion of the man who had been one of the twentieth century's most notorious atheists. Unbelievers decried his conversion as absurd, with many claiming or at least implying—as Richard Dawkins did in his book *The God Delusion*—that the aged Flew converted only because of senility or some other type of mental decline.

What was the cause for Flew's change of mind? For years he claimed that he, like the Greek philosopher Socrates, would have to follow the evidence wherever it led. For nearly his whole life, he believed that the evidence pointed to unbelief as the most logical and rational worldview to be had. Over the course of a couple of decades, Flew debated with some of the brightest minds Christianity had to offer. One such fellow was Thomas B. Warren, an intellectual titan and a member of the churches of Christ. Another was New Testament scholar Gary Habermas, who defeated Flew in a debate on the resurrection of Christ held in 1985.

Flew's method is both an admirable one and an intellectually respectable one. In order to discover truth, we have to follow the evidence wherever it leads. This isn't always an easy task. Sometimes we have pet theories, or draw conclusions that we don't want to concede. We may be in competition with someone else, or we may just be uncomfortable with the results. When it comes to spiritual matters, it is often the latter that is the case.

It is a sad reality that many people do not want God to exist. Many deny God's existence because it provides them with a feeling of liberation. Aldous Huxley once commented that he did not want the world to have meaning because a lack of meaning provided liberation from morality. This freedom from being bound by morality, in turn, freed him from interference in his sexual proclivities. A quick look in the relationship advice columns of the morning paper will find many who would agree with him.

If we are to find real truth, we have to follow the evidence. We must be willing to distance ourselves from our cherished beliefs, because those beliefs may or may not be true. We have to look at the evidence and compare our beliefs to reality. Do they really reflect life as it is? Or do they simply exist because they represent what we want?

In this book we are going to look at a number of different areas in which the evidence points to a Creator of this universe, a God who has left His indelible mark on creation and described Himself in His autobiography. We will explore a number of areas, some scientific, some philosophical. But above all else, we must first have a burning passion to discover the truth.

The truth is out there and can be discovered by human beings. I hope you will join me in following the facts wherever they might lead.

Truth 1

We Can Know the Truth

Pontius Pilate had a knack for irritating people. He was an unpopular fellow with both his superiors and his subordinates. One of his first acts as governor of Judea was to take money from the temple treasury to pay for the construction of an aqueduct, which did not sit well with his Jewish subjects. After repeatedly irritating Emperor Tiberius, he attempted to smooth things over by building a temple in the emperor's honor. It was little more than a Band-Aid™ on a gaping political wound. He stayed in constant trouble with the Roman emperor and would eventually be exiled to Gaul (modern day France), where he committed suicide.

Years before his tragic demise, Pilate had the opportunity of a lifetime. The very Son of God stood in front of him, having been up all night sitting through an illegal trial. He was marched before the Roman governor to answer the charges laid against Him by His fellow countrymen. During the conversation, Pilate looked Jesus in the eye and asked Him if the charges against Him were true. After receiving a response that eluded his understanding, Pilate responded by throwing his hands in the air and asking, "What is truth?"

(John 18:38). In a moment of exasperation, the troubled Roman governor spoke for the hundreds of millions who have asked the same question ever since then.

We live in an age where truth is like a wax nose, able to be shaped to suit the taste of the observer. Christianity has been hit especially hard by this recent turn of events. At one time, people assumed that truth could indeed be known. First it took the form of trust in an authority figure like a king or priest. Later it was faith in human reason, to which the philosophers after the Enlightenment appealed as a way to discover truth. Finally, humanity dispensed with any outside source of truth whatsoever, preferring instead to keep it an internal affair. Now we manufacture our own truth, custom-fit to order.

What many people do not realize is that Truth 2.0 isn't rational. It isn't logical. In short, it's a deficiency in sound thinking. On the surface, it sounds magnanimous to have individual truth. That way no one ever has to fight or argue. We simply say, "You've got your truth, I've got my truth," and suddenly everyone can agree to disagree because no one has the right to tell anyone else that he is wrong. But if we are going to look at reality and try to understand reality as it is, there are judgments that have to be made. Some people are right, and some people are wrong. It boils down to the question, "What is truth?"

In discussing the very important matter of Christianity and the reasons why it should be taken seriously, we have to begin with an understanding of worldviews.

It's All Relative

I once had a friend with whom I attended a Christian high school. I caught up with him years after we graduated. He invited me over to his house and told me that he had embraced Buddhism. He carefully explained that while attending a Christian college, he took a Bible class in which the last question on the final exam asked him to explain why another religion was wrong. He told me that it was at that point he realized that Christianity was exclusivistic and intolerant. He searched for what he thought was a better way to look at the realm of belief and finally settled on Buddhism. With enthusiasm he explained that religion is like a mountain. Different faiths are like different paths to the top where God can be found. Some paths may have a gentle grade, while others are much steeper. Some paths might be like taking a stroll; others require an arduous climb. But every path that leads to the top of the mountain has access to God. He told me with increasing excitement that each person takes a unique path to God. And even though two people might take the same route, their footsteps will be different along the way. Each individual's faith is uniquely satisfying for that person. And we accept every path because we're all trying to get to the same place. Speechless, I looked at him in sadness, desperately searching in vain for something I could say that would counteract his thoroughly relativistic worldview.

Everyone has a worldview. A worldview is how a person views the world, the glasses through which they see and interpret reality. Some people are religious, and interpret the information of the world around them in light of the existence of their god, God, or gods. Others are not religious; so much of what they see around them is interpreted in a naturalistic manner. There are many different kinds of worldviews out there, including tolerant religious pluralists, paranoid conspiracy theorists, and everything in between.

In our current postmodern age, truth has become much more flexible than at any other time in the past. In the pre-modern age, people generally believed they could trust the authorities and the experts. This changed in the mid-1800's, ushering in the modern period, where the average person was thought to have sufficient powers of reason to rely on his own ability to discover truth. Reason (with a capital "R") became the most important principle, and as long as a person's thinking sought out and operated according to the universal principle of Reason, then proper belief would be the natural result. Science gained a great deal of authority as scientists became the final arbiters of truth. Also during this time, emphasis on empirical evidence obtained by the five senses assumed vital importance. A belief developed that only through science could a person find truth. In the postmodern age, roughly the mid-twentieth century onward, no authority is trusted, whether a human figure or a universal principle. There is no authority, except the authority each individual creates.

Postmodernism makes absolute truth an elusive commodity. Truth has essentially become nothing more than personal opinion in masquerade. It is subjective truth, shaped by the individual. There is little appeal to evidence, universal standards, or objective data. This kind of thinking is what Francis Schaeffer described as having one's feet planted firmly in mid-air. Without any foundation or guiding principles, how does one truly know anything?

History is full of one-liners, famous quotes that are still used today though they may have been first uttered centuries or even millennia ago. Philosophy has its fair share of pithy statements, such as the German philosopher Friedrich Nietzsche's famous declaration "God is dead." Socrates said, "Question everything." The ancient philosopher Parmenides said, "Whatever is, is." (And he's famous for it. Go figure.)

One such statement that concerns us here is a classic from Rene Descartes: "I think, therefore I am." Descartes was a French mathematician and philosopher who wanted to discover a way to truly know truth. He concocted a brilliantly simple plan: doubt everything until you get down to the most fundamental truth that cannot be doubted, then use this point as your starting place. As he whittled away reality with his philosophical knife, he finally arrived at something he could not dismiss: his ability to think. Most people would just pass over this idea as something that is common sense. But to Descartes it was a powerful idea. His ability to reason was the one thing that could not be doubted because doubt verified his ability to think. The fact that he could think about thinking meant that his ability to think, and therefore his existence, was an undeniable truth.

That's Just Your Interpretation

We live in a postmodern culture. Postmodernism is a viewpoint that there is no such thing as absolute truth when it comes to ideas; there are only interpretations. Ultimately, what you and I think is nothing more than an opinion and the individualistic way we see the world around us. The relativist claims that universal truth in the realm of ideas does not exist. There are only subjective opinions and interpretations. But Descartes was on to something when he found the very thing he could not deny. There is incontrovertible truth to be had, as long as we're willing to put forth the mental effort to find it.

America is a melting pot. We have a wide range of cultures represented in American society today all coming together to form one nation. In the consciousness of our country there is almost an implicit understanding of diversity, which is expressed by the motto *e pluribus unum* ("out of many, one"). Along with this diversity in ethnicity and culture is a diversity in worldviews. In the postmodern society in which we live, some believe that all viewpoints should be not only tolerated but celebrated. Why judge someone else? Why not allow all people to have their own truths?

When worldviews come into conflict, one means of escape or evasion is the catch phrase, "That's just your interpretation." Even when the case for truth is carefully laid down, some will dismiss it as being nothing more than one person's perspective. Was Nietzsche correct when he said, "There are no facts, only interpretations"?

The phrase, "That's just your interpretation," is something of a catch-22 because the person using it considers his own viewpoint to be much more than just an interpretation. The speaker usually believes his own opinion conforms to fact or reality while another's does not. In essence, he is stating that everyone's opinion is relative except for his own. Rarely does anyone offer what he firmly believes as nothing more than one possibility among many. The best way to confront this kind of evasion would be to ask very simple questions: Where do you think I am misinterpreting the facts? What are your reasons for disagreeing with my interpretation? In your opinion, what is the correct interpretation?

Much of our culture is based more on feeling than on thinking. We don't ever want people to feel badly about themselves. When high school students flunk, we give them a graduation certificate so they won't feel bad for having failed to get a diploma. We make policies of evaluation easier so that fewer students will fail their coursework. We promote students to the next grade level even though they haven't earned the grades to get there. The message our culture is sending is shockingly clear: we will tolerate failure at thinking, but we don't want to feel badly for it.

When we read what Scripture has to say, we immediately discover that faith is not concerned merely with feeling. It is also concerned with truth. We separate knowledge from belief. Knowledge is knowing actual facts that correctly conform to fact or reality, while belief is often synonymous with feeling. If I believe something is true, I am stating a matter of opinion. If I know something is true, then there is certainty and confidence.

Evidence

Some sections of Christianity today have divorced themselves from thinking and examining the evidence. Faith, for some, is a matter of feeling without any need to engage the mind. Some of the most potent criticisms of Christianity stem from the mistaken belief that Christians do not think about anything or evaluate any evidence, but merely rely on "blind faith."

Modern culture believes that empirical knowledge—the kind derived from one's senses—is the only true knowledge. Science has staked a claim on this variety of knowledge, in part because that is the nature of the discipline. Scientists must be able to observe and reproduce the events observed. That is the very nature of the scientific method. While this is fine for the sciences, it cannot be applied across the board to all kinds of knowledge. If a person always insisted on empirical knowledge for everything, he would never trust a newspaper, historian, or nightly news anchor. In short, he could never trust anything outside his own experience.

Trusting other evidence is much of the problem behind science's supposed refutation of religion. While secular science insists on empirical knowledge, those very scientists do not limit themselves to that kind of knowledge. They themselves rely on published reports, experiments, and other forms of data. They trust in the ability of other scientists to formulate theories and conduct proper experiments. In short, scientists have a kind of faith in other scientists.

Logic is the basic foundation for human thinking. It helps us determine what is meaningful and what is meaningless. It is a potent force on the battlefield of ideas. In some cases, we can be our own worst enemies by using self-refuting arguments. Examples are "We cannot know for certain that anything exists" (you would have to exist to make this statement), "we cannot know truth" (which is a truth claim), or "all truth is relative" (which is an absolute truth claim). Some critics are fond of starting from a naturalistic viewpoint that accepts only scientific evidence as a test of truth. In other words, "Only things that are scientifically verifiable can be true." It probably does not occur to those making this statement that they are asserting the statement as a truth, but one cannot perform a scientific test on a statement or assertion of fact. It is a self-defeating argument.

Many critics like to claim that Christians avoid evidence at all costs. In truth, the Bible actually appeals to empirical evidence. Take the miracles, for example. These were tangible, visible signs that accompanied the messages of prophets and apostles. Not only that, but the apostles Peter (2 Peter 1:16), John (1 John 1:1, 2), and Paul (1 Corinthians 15:5-8) all stake their claims on eyewitness evidence for the risen Christ. Christian apologists have followed in the apostles' footsteps. Believers from every field of science have investigated facts that have led them to conclude that God exists.

Is Religion the Product of Experience?

When it comes to religion, some critics state that a person's beliefs are simply the product of his background or upbringing. Modern atheists have used that argument in attacking Christianity, stating that if a person was born in a religious context, he would naturally adopt that religion. Likewise, in a scientifically enlightened world where religion does not exist, no one would ever abandon reason to adopt religious superstition.

While it is true that one's personal experience shapes his worldview, the critic is really missing the point. He is beginning with the assumption that his own worldview is the correct one. He is also assuming that being raised in a religious context is wrong unless it agrees with his. The religious pluralist will argue against exclusive religions, while the atheist will argue against all religions. The important thing to remember is that just because a person adopts the dominant religion in his or her context does not have any bearing on the truth of that religion.

If a person grew up in Nazi Germany, chances are they would have been part of the Hitler Youth. The same goes for anyone growing up in the Soviet Union, who would likely have been a part of the All-Union Leninist Young Communist League. But that has no bearing on which government is truer. As philosopher Paul Copan puts it, "Just because a diversity of political opinions has existed in the history of the world doesn't obstruct us from evaluating one political system as superior to its rivals."[i] The same goes for religion. A person growing up in a Hindu, Muslim, Christian, or Buddhist culture and adopting the dominant religion says nothing about how true that religion is. No one can hide behind ignorance, because God has left an indelible signature upon His creation (Psalm 19:1-6; Romans 1:18-20).

Religious belief as a product of experience makes for a poor argument, although it is one frequently used by critics. Popular Christian apologist Amy Orr-Ewing says, "No other intellectual discipline would accept such a superficial approach to truth. Why accept it here, when it comes to a fundamental belief system?"[ii]

So What?

It is *en vogue* to claim that objective truth is dead. In his book, *The Closing of the American Mind*, Allan Bloom writes, "there is one thing a professor can be absolutely certain of: almost every student entering the university believes, or says he believes, that truth is relative...The students, of course, cannot defend their opinion. It is something with which they have been indoctrinated."[iii] Critics, especially those from a more radical postmodern bend, will claim that there is no such thing as objective truth or knowledge. But look carefully at that statement. The very statement "there is no such thing as objective truth" is stated as an objective truth. It refutes itself. Unlike beauty, truth is not in the eye of the beholder. The careful observer will quickly be able to see through the blue smoke and mirrors of pseudo-philosophical language that Christianity's critics employ. It often takes only a short while before the contradictions become exposed. All a person usually needs is some good critical thinking skills.

In the end, we cannot escape truth. We cannot deny it, and we would contradict ourselves if we did. "There is no such thing as truth" is, after all, a truth claim. Even radical skeptics who think that all truth is subjective will disagree with those who do not share their opinion, and disagreement implies that someone is not holding beliefs that are objectively true. Truth is assumed by every worldview, even those that deny it exists. Unfortunately, such people are either unable or unwilling to see the contradictions their denial creates.

There is a world of evidence around us. According to the laws of logic and rational thinking, there is only one true way to interpret it. That is, there is one reality and any description of it is either true or false. There is no other alternative.

Jesus told others that He is the only way to God (John 14:6). To a culture consumed with tolerance, this seems like an incredibly arrogant statement. Our society is conditioned to think of truth as something that exists purely because we believe in it. If Jesus' statement actually conforms to reality—that there is a God and the death of Jesus Christ is the only way to enjoy eternal blessedness with Him—then not only is Jesus' statement true; it is a moral imperative. If Jesus' statement correctly represents the facts, then every human being must accept it as true or face the direst of consequences.

The more we try to escape the truth, the more we end up affirming it. As we continue our walk through evidence that has compelled the greatest skeptics to become believers in the Bible and the God who inspired its authors, I urge you to keep an open mind. Don't take everything I say at face value. Be skeptical if you will. Christians have no fear of the facts, and I am confident that once you investigate them you will become more and more aware of the one responsible for the creation of this wide wonderful universe. But before we get to the one who started it all, we have to go back to the beginning.

Truth 2

The Universe Had a Creator

Human beings are concerned about the big questions in life. Why am I here? What is my purpose? What does life really mean? We want to know about our personal origins and our place on planet Earth. We ask our parents about what happened before we were born to get a sense of connection with the past. We trace our family histories to get a larger perspective because our past has a direct bearing on who we are. A large part of our identity involves our origins and our place in the world right now. We realize that we are a part of something much larger, and understanding the interconnectedness of our experience helps us understand ourselves.

One of the questions people often ask is "How did I get here?" Of course, this is not a simple question of birth. The question is bigger, more existential. We are asking, "What is the ultimate cause for my existence?" We want to know *why* we are here. Why we feel emotions. Whether our souls exist or if we are just ghosts in the machine. Are we just a figment of someone's imagination or a character in someone else's dream?

When we ask "Why am I here?" we are getting back to the origin of everything. We are a part of the universe; and in asking about our place in the cosmos, we are implicitly asking where the universe originated. We want to know why everything is the way it is and how it came to be that way. Knowing that goes a long way to helping us establish our identities, understand who we are, and realize our place and purpose in this crazy roller coaster ride called life.

Not a Chance

When we stop to think about how this universe came to be, we have three options available to us. The universe: (1) appeared out of nothing, (2) has always existed, or (3) was created by someone. Critics of the faith won't allow the third option because according to secular science, the divine doesn't exist. So which of the two remaining options is it? Did the universe appear from nowhere, or has it always been? Actually, neither.

The first assertion, that the universe came from nothing, is a logical absurdity even in the eyes of science itself. An important understanding of modern science is the basic principle of cause and effect. Every effect must have not only a cause but a sufficient cause. So how did the universe appear from nothing? Very simple: chance. The hero of the godless story of the universe is time. Given enough time, anything can happen. Even when the chances are remote, enough time supposedly makes everything possible. Unfortunately, chance by itself is not an adequate explanation for the universe.

We often hear that things happen "by chance." In everything ranging from the existence of the universe to the likelihood of life evolving on earth, chance is responsible for everything existing. Unfortunately, this is one of the most prolific modern myths in American culture. In his book *Not a Chance*, philosopher and Christian apologist R.C. Sproul examines the idea of chance. He says, chance has no power to do anything. It is cosmically, totally, consummately impotent ... chance has no power to do anything because it simply is not anything. It has no power because it has no being.[i]

It is "by chance" that the universe came to be or that life exists on earth. But chance is nothing more than a mathematical probability. As Sproul says, it has no power to do, make, or be *anything*. It is nothing more than a concept or idea. If the universe exists, then it has to derive its existence from something else. Chance is not a suitable candidate.

The alternative to a universe that just pops into existence is one that has existed for eternity. In the immortal words of the late astronomer Carl Sagan, "The Cosmos is all that is or ever was or ever will be."[ii] Many scientists theorize that the universe has always existed, perpetually created in a Big Bang which creates a new universe until gravitational forces slowly pull it back in to collapse in upon itself once more. Once the mass becomes a super-dense ball of matter, it explodes in another Big Bang event. This Oscillating Universe theory is a popular one, but many acknowledge that there are difficulties with it. Could our universe have existed forever? Newton's Second Law of Thermodynamics argues against it.

The Second Law of Thermodynamics, also called the law of entropy, states that everything is running down. The available energy in the universe is being depleted even as you read this sentence. That means that if the universe's available energy is being exhausted, then there is a time when it will be completely gone. If the universe really existed forever, the energy contained within it would have been used up long ago. The idea that the universe has always existed, called the Steady State theory, cannot be true.

Another argument that cannot be true is the Oscillating Universe theory, also called the cyclic model. Some would argue that the universe is going through cycles beginning with a Big Bang and ending when gravity pulls the universe back into a single point again.

This is followed by another Big Bang, creating another universe. Current research shows that the matter in the universe is expanding too quickly to collapse, however. Gravity is not strong enough to pull everything back together. Even if it did, the collapse would result in a Big Crunch. There wouldn't be enough energy left to fuel another Big Bang.

So where did the universe originate? According to the laws of physics, it hasn't been here forever. We also know that it cannot just pop into being or create itself. So if we revisit our three options for the universe's existence listed above, we can cross the first two off our list. The only remaining option is to say that God created the universe. The fact that it is *here* means that something or someone else is responsible for it. The idea that an outside power had to bring the earth into existence sounds curiously like the opening verse of the Bible, "In the beginning, God created the heavens and the earth" (Genesis 1:1).

The idea that God causes things to be seems to be implied from His very name in the Old Testament. The sacred covenant name Yahweh or YHWH in the Hebrew Bible has its origins in the Hebrew word *ehyeh*, meaning "I am." When used in the third person, it can be translated as "he is" or "he causes to be." It may also be translated in a sense indicating causality, such as "I am the one who causes [or calls into being]." God is the source of being, and anything else that exists is because of Him.

While other theories fall short or contradict some known law of nature, the Bible is logically and scientifically consistent. If God has the power to create, then the universe has a sufficient cause for its existence. Making this statement does not violate logic or any natural laws. Another question is this: Did God create from nothing? The term for "to create" found in Genesis is the Hebrew term *bara'*, which is used only of God's activity. There are other words used for concepts such as fashioning, working, or making, but *bara'* is used of God alone. It is a special word for creation but does not necessarily mean that God created from nothing. Other passages do indicate that God created from nothing, however. The writer of Hebrews says, "[T]he universe was created by the word of God, so that what is seen was not made out of things that are visible" (Hebrews 11:3). Long ago, everything began to exist when God spoke that first divine word.

Science and the Christian Worldview

After seeing that pure chance cannot be responsible for the existence of the universe, the issue remains: How does one harmonize religion and science? In the modern media, especially among Christianity's critics, religion is seen as an archaic leftover of human culture that is better left in the dustbin of history. Science has come along to replace it. It offers rational answers superior to religion's superstitious explanations. Can oil and water ever mix?

The uneasy relationship between religion and science is the result of adopting a purely naturalistic worldview. From the beginning it is deemed that the supernatural doesn't exist, so with one fell swoop religion is deprived of a seat at the negotiating table. No explanation for why the supernatural cannot happen is ever offered. It "just doesn't."

The march of scientific progress hasn't refuted Scripture as much as critics would like. With the ongoing discoveries made we have found that the universe is remarkably anthropocentric (human-centered). In fact, the anthropic principle states that the universe appears to be far too human-friendly to simply be the product of a cosmic accident. Numerous requirements in the areas of chemistry, geology, hydrology, physics, biology, genetics, and a host of other scientific specializations are absolutely necessary for even the smallest organism to survive, much less larger ones like animals and people.

More than a dozen universal constants must remain fixed in order to provide a universal framework in which life can exist. Many of these constants are necessary to maintain important chemical bonds, gravity, and have the sun be able to provide energy for life on earth. It is this number of fine-tuned constants that permits life to exist on Earth. Additionally, there are even more individual properties of our planet that make life possible. The orbit of the moon, the density of Earth, and its distance from the sun are just a few of the dozens of details that are precisely calibrated for life to exist on this planet. If any one of these were changed by the smallest measurable amount, life on Earth would be impossible.

Even skeptics have commented on the conspicuously precise conditions on Earth that allow living things to exist. As Brad Lemley wrote in *Discover* magazine, "The universe is unlikely. Very unlikely. Deeply, shockingly unlikely."[iii] In the same article, Lemley quotes Cambridge astronomer and skeptic Martin Rees, who says that if the basic, fundamental properties of the universe were altered "even to the tiniest degree, there would be no stars, no complex elements, no life" and that any genuine consideration of these fundamental forces makes the existence of the universe "unlikely to an absurd degree."[iv]

The fine-tuning of the universe immediately calls to mind Paul's words to the church in Rome: "For his invisible attributes, namely, his eternal power and divine nature, have been clearly perceived, ever since the creation of the world, in the things that have been made" (Romans 1:20). Although the apostle did not know about the laws of physics or universal constants, he knew that creation itself bears witness to the one who created it. As science delves ever deeper into the basic understanding of our universe, we uncover more and more evidence that what we see around us simply cannot exist by chance.

How About a Date?

Ever since the Enlightenment, secular science has been encroaching on the Bible. This is not to say that Christians should be anti-science. The study of science shows that something had to create the universe. It also shows that great evidence exists for the existence of God. Further, sciences like archaeology (which will be discussed in chapter 5) demonstrate the trustworthiness of Scripture. Christians should never fear science, but welcome it.

Like any other field of study, the sciences are subject to interpretation in varying degrees. This is true even in sciences such as geology, which is one of the key fields in the debate of the age of Earth. Many scientists believe that Earth is about 4.5 billion years old, based on results from radiometric dating. This method of determining the ages of rocks in Earth's crust is taken as absolute proof of the extreme age of the planet, but there are significant problems with the method.

One example of the failure of radiometric dating involves geological samples taken from eruptions of Mount Ngauruhoe in New Zealand. It is one of the most active volcanoes in recent history. It had major eruptions in 1948, 1955, and 1975. Samples of the volcanic rocks created in the eruptions were sent to the Geochron Laboratories in Massachusetts for dating. The lab was not told anything about the suspected age of the rocks or where they were collected. The results showed that the rocks were as much as 3.5 million years old.[v] Volcanic rocks from the Mount Saint Helens eruption in 1980 sent to the same lab yielded similar results. The lab said the newly-formed rocks were several hundreds of thousands of years old when they had only been formed ten years previously.[vi] The dating methods used to provide an age of millions of years for the planet clearly have their problems. Evidence suggests that current dating methods can and do suffer from monumental failure.

Similar embarrassing episodes have occurred recently in paleontology. Evolutionary theory is heavily dependent upon dating methods that supposedly demonstrate the Earth is billions of years old. Scientists claim these dating methods provide absolute evidence. But environmental factors and starting assumptions make a huge difference in the results of these tests. In an unthreatening environment, any scientist will acknowledge that radiometric dating is imprecise. If the subject of God or creationism is brought up, however, the wagons quickly circle and specialists rush to defend the universal acceptance of these methods.

In March 2004, scientists from Montana State University discovered a dinosaur fossil still containing soft tissue. In March 2005, National Geographic reported the discovery of a *Tyrannosaurus rex*.[vii] When moving the bones, the thigh bone was too big to be lifted by helicopter, so it was deliberately broken into two sections in the field. The scientists were surprised to find soft tissue inside the fossil. Upon closer inspection, the specialists found blood vessels and even blood cells within the soft, spongy tissues. The evidence suggested that the fossil had been preserved very recently. Rather than accept a recent date for the fossil, Mary Schweitzer (the paleontologist who reported the find in the academic literature) said that scientists are still trying to come up with a model of fossilization that preserves soft tissues.[viii] Rather than reexamine the dating used to determine the age of the dinosaurs, the first response was to question the evidence. Experts are still trying to determine a way that soft tissues could be preserved for tens of millions of years. The simplest and best approach is to avoid special pleading and accept the reality that dinosaurs walked the earth fairly recently.

More Than a Feeling

Faith is popularly defined as believing in something you know isn't true, which is more or less a kind of deluded self-deception. A less hostile but equally unflattering definition of faith is belief in something for which there is no proof. True biblical faith is very different from its popular definitions. Faith is trust or reliance upon what one knows to be true. Unlike ancient myths which didn't care to present historical facts, the Bible consistently grounds itself in historical reality. Many times even pagans did not believe their own myths really happened. That is not the same case for Christianity.

Christians came by faith because they had seen real events. In 1 Corinthians 15:4-9, Paul said that Jesus appeared to all the apostles and that five hundre witnesses had seen Him in a single sitting

(v. 6). Peter (2 Peter 1:16) and John (1 John 1:1-4) also claimed to be eyewitnesses. These men did not ground their faith in fanciful stories, but in reality.

A person can know many things without having firsthand knowledge. George Washington was the first president of the United States; we believe this even though we never met him. We know that countries outside the United States exist, though we may have never visited them. Even if we look at a globe or see pictures or video from one of these places, how do we really know they exist? Human beings work off of reliable testimony. Given the weight and quality of the evidence from various sources, we can determine that Washington really was president and that other places outside our travels really do exist.

When we look at the concept that the universe had a creator, we are forced to acknowledge that the universe got here somehow. It couldn't have popped into existence, and it couldn't have created itself. Both ideas are logically absurd. That means that something else—a greater power—had to be responsible. It isn't just faith that says the universe had a creator. So do the facts. It is an undeniable fact that the universe had to have an agent who generated it. This is an uncomfortable issue for unbelievers, but it is one that every human must deal with if we are going to look at all the evidence.

Who is this creator? Surveying human history, there are many ideas about which deity is responsible for the creation of the universe. In the next chapter we'll make a case for the one who is most often credited with the accomplishment of creation.

Conclusion

In the end, Christians have no reason to be worried about propaganda from secular science, because there are plenty of scientists who believe in God. Although their voices are not often heard due to ideological discrimination, that does not change the fact that there is a divine alternative to godless theories. In the end, we can summarize several points that the evidence makes:

- According to scientific laws, the universe had a beginning.
- The delicately balanced universe gives every appearance of being designed to support life, especially human life.
- No current naturalistic explanation fits the evidence for a godless universe.
- Current evidence creates many problems for a 4.6 billion-year-old date for Earth.
- Science cannot offer proof of the non-existence of God or the illegitimacy of the Christian worldview, because it is capable of addressing only the physical, not the supernatural.

The scientific evidence that we have clearly points to an origin of the universe. The design and complexity found within it argue that this origin was intentional. And if something is intentional, then there must be intent, which requires a person. The only person able to create a universe is God. So there we have it, the picture of creation just as we see it in the Bible. In the beginning.

Truth 3

God Exists

Two boys were talking one day. One of them looked at a tree and remarked, "I wonder who made the tree?" The other boy answered, "God made it." The first boy looked at an unusual rock and asked the same question. "Oh yeah, well who made the rock?" His friend answered, "God made it, too." Mulling over the answer for a few moments, the first boy came up with a new question, "Okay, who made God?" The second boy thought about it for a moment before announcing, "God made Himself!"

Believe it or not, this is the same kind of question millions are asking at this very moment. Who made God? It's actually a valid question. Did mankind just create God? Is He a figment of our imaginations like the tooth fairy or the Loch Ness monster? Perhaps a kind of cosmic grandfather that comforts us in the hard times of life? Or a kind of divine Santa Claus who grants our wishes if we pray earnestly enough?

Sigmund Freud was Jewish and anything but a believer. He viewed the God of the Bible as simply one version of a sky deity invented by mankind to help him understand the unexplained and cope with life. For instance, mankind is powerless in the face of the tornado or the forest fire. Even so, he cannot stomach the idea of being blown about by the random winds of chance and fate. Rather than submit to his place of powerlessness and relative unimportance in the world, man invents a deity to help him control his environment. While he cannot stop the tornado, he envisions a god that can. And he can pray to this god who is able to stop the tornado. In the end, man has power over the elements because his god will listen to his prayers and act on his behalf like a cosmic bodyguard, protecting him from things from which he cannot protect himself.

In our present age of extreme skepticism, how does one make a case for God? All too often believers just accept some form of *fideism* (pronounced FEE-day-izm). This is the reliance upon a kind of blind faith and a dismissal of external evidence. "Just take it on faith" could ably serve as the slogan of fideism. Some will go so far as to say that a person needs to take a "leap of faith." Here we have the picture of someone leaping off the edge into the inky blackness of the unknown, hoping against all hope that someone is there to catch them. While this is a position that many people take, from the standpoint of faith it is not only intellectually lazy but spiritually foolish. Better arguments can be had in the defense of God's existence.

The Cosmological Argument

The origins of the cosmological argument can be found in Greek philosophy, although it has been popular with Christian theologians for centuries. After going through several stages of development, one of the most popular forms of the argument is the kalam cosmological argument. It states

Everything that exists must have a cause for its existence.
The universe began to exist; therefore,
The universe has a cause for its existence.

The first premise goes back to the work of Aristotle who argued for a first cause of everything that he called the Unmoved Mover. The basic concept didn't originate with Aristotle; he merely recognized it as many do today. Whether it is the Christian explanation that God created it (Genesis 1:1, 2) or the secular scientific explanation that it was the result of the Big Bang, almost everyone agrees that there was a point at which our universe began to be. Something is here right now, so something else has to be responsible for that something to get here.

This premise is fairly easy to defend. The second Law of Thermodynamics—also known as the law of entropy—states that everything in the universe is moving from a state of order to a state of disorder. The universe has only a finite amount of energy. If the universe is infinitely old, then the universe would have burned through all its energy long ago.

Some try to side-step this argument by offering the Oscillating Universe theory as an explanation. In the beginning, a tiny ball of "stuff" detonated in the Big Bang, creating the universe. That tiny ball came from the last universe that collapsed upon itself, compacted by gravity until it reached critical mass, creating the latest version of the universe. This doesn't really answer anything. Our question is not "how did the universe get here?" but "where did the universe come from?" Those are two very different questions. We want to know where the "stuff" that makes up our universe originated, not how it got into its latest form. There are two problems that physicists now recognize: (1) the universe is too big for gravity to cause it to collapse, and (2) if it could collapse, it wouldn't explode and create another one.

The second premise is that the universe began to exist. Unless we are willing to claim (as a few do) that all of reality is an illusion, then the existence of the universe is quite obvious. If it were simply an illusion, there would be little worth in debating the nature of existence!

The conclusion is that the universe has a cause for its existence. Obviously, if something exists, then something greater had to generate it. The idea that the universe just popped into being is absurd, as is the idea that the universe could be self-created. In order for something to *be*, something else has to give it the power of *being*. Christians and atheists alike agree that time, space, and matter did not exist prior to the point of origin for the universe. In that case, the origin of the universe has to be timeless and immaterial. It also cannot be subject to the physical laws of the universe, which require time, space, and matter.

This cause must have had a reason for acting, which requires decision-making and free will. These attributes mean that the cause must have been personal in nature. If this cause is ultimately personal, then obviously it must point to a person. While the cosmological argument does not specifically stipulate that the cause of the universe's existence is the God of the Bible, it is certainly a good fit with the evidence.

The Teleological Argument

The cosmological argument for the existence of God isn't the only one out there. A second is the teleological argument, known also as the argument from design. This argument states that the evidence of design in nature is too great to be ascribed to chance and natural law. From the greatest expanses of the cosmos down to the smallest intricacies on the molecular level, dozens of universal constants keep the universe functioning fairly predictably.

Closely aligned with the teleological argument is the anthropic principle. This observes that the universe almost seems to be custom fit for life, especially human life. This includes the precise distance from Earth to the Sun for the right temperature, as well as the axis and rotation of Earth.

The apparent design of the universe has not escaped the attention of atheists. Figures such as Richard Dawkins, perhaps the most notable evolutionist in the world today, have argued that while the universe appears to have design, this is merely an illusion. He doesn't back up his claims with much evidence, other than the simple assertion that appearances can be deceiving. This may be true in some cases, but it is impossible to defend the idea that every occurrence of design is illusory.

Some have found the design argument so compelling that it has brought them out of atheism. The best known example is Antony Flew, one of the most famous atheists of the twentieth century. Despite having eloquently and passionately argued against theism for nearly his entire life, he was later won over in 2004 to belief in God. Although his definition of God is clearly not the God of the Bible, he nevertheless believes that there must be something at work to have generated the sprawling universe in all its beautiful complexity.

The argument for design is a tricky one, but is better than the cosmological argument. It argues for a creator, but cannot specify who that creator is. We know that this creator must be very powerful, knowledgeable, personal, and good, but we cannot know his exact identity. Though it isn't conclusive, the argument is a powerful one. Secular voices claim that the universe is random and impersonal. But evidence for a creator implies that there is both purpose and personality involved in creating something like this universe in which we live.

William Paley (1743-1805) is famous for his watchmaker argument. Let's say we find a watch lying on the ground. We pick it up and examine it closely. Its intricate machinery and precise design tell us that someone made it. Obviously, something as complex and purposeful as a watch must have a watchmaker who created it. The same is true for the universe.

The Bible claims that God deliberately and purposefully created the world, and science seems to affirm this fact. Complexity and order cannot be the result of randomness and chaos. Design and purpose are effects that require sufficient causes. God is often excluded from consideration, however. It is quite popular for critics to start from the standpoint of philosophical naturalism, which says that nothing supernatural can be considered. But we must also realize that it is impossible to defend that viewpoint. It's one thing to say, "Science can't detect the supernatural, so we aren't sure it exists." It's quite another to say, "Even though science can't detect the supernatural, we are certain it doesn't exist." The former is a legitimate admission; the latter is not.

The immensely intricate design of the world suggests that someone is responsible. Though some critics argue that nature sometimes has the *illusion* of design that can be explained by natural means, this does not take into account the immensely minute fine-tuning of the universe for the existence of life as we know it. Even unbelievers note how the universe seems to argue for an intelligence behind its inner workings. They deny the existence of God and are reluctant to affirm that this organization opens the door for the argument from design, but the facts speak for themselves. In a universe delicately balanced for life, one must ask whether it is better to believe in odds that are beyond the range of possibility or in a God who set everything in motion.

The Moral Argument

Although the existence of evil, pain, and suffering is often seen as the most powerful argument against the existence of God (which will be examined in greater detail in chapter 8), the ability to distinguish the difference between good and evil is also seen as evidence in favor of God's existence. As we will see later, evil is tragic; but there is a reason for it.

John Leo reports, "Several years ago, a college professor in upstate New York reported that 10 percent to 20 percent of his students could not bring themselves to criticize the Nazi extermination of Europe's Jews. Some students expressed personal distaste for what the Nazis did. But they were not willing to say that the Nazis were wrong, since no culture can be judged from the outside and no individual can challenge the moral worldview of another."[i] Although the students expressed their disagreement with the Holocaust, they did not believe they had a foundation to argue that Hitler's actions were evil. They aren't alone.

Denying absolute standards of right and wrong is comfortable for some, and others just dispense with the argument altogether. But what if a person were to be confronted by a murderer or rapist in a dark alley with no witnesses? I doubt very seriously that the denial of absolute right and wrong would last very long under that kind of duress. Speculating from an ivory tower is one thing. It is something else entirely when real life intrudes.

Murder, torture, and rape are only a few examples of evils that anyone should deny. The average person is equipped with the moral faculties to recognize evil for what it is (cf. Rom. 2:14, 15). Our question is this: what is the origin of those faculties?

Theologians and philosophers suggest that the innate sense of morals possessed by virtually all human beings comes from God. If there are absolute morals then they had to come from somewhere. Humans differ from the members of the animal kingdom in that we feel guilt for wrongdoing. Whether a minor accident or a catastrophic event occurs, people have recognition of responsibility and fault. The animal kingdom does not. Lions do not agonize over the ethical implications of eating a gazelle or how its death will affect its family or the members of its community. The lion knows two states of being: hunger and satisfaction. The gazelle is merely a means to an end.

Unlike animals, human beings appear to have an innate sense of right and wrong. Professional ethics, medical ethics, and business ethics are just a few areas in which human beings try to quantify right and wrong as it applies to each, usually without any reference to the Bible. Indeed, the wrongs identified in each are not only frowned upon; in some cases, they're criminal. But what is the cause for this intrinsic ability to recognize and quantify right and wrong that is unparalleled among the animals?

Some evolutionists claim that things like morality and altruism could have evolved over time. Because these apply to behavior, they are beyond the purview of evolutionary biology. While biology can speak to the physical features of an organism, evolution cannot explain why it is inappropriate to talk negatively about the appearance of a co-worker, forbid a psychiatrist to accept a personal gift from a client, or permit theft and even murder among animals but not humans. It is also problematic that all people, even those who recognize no God or higher power, can still be good, moral people.

Bertrand Russell once wrote, "We feel that the man who brings widespread happiness at the expense of misery to himself is a better man than the man who brings unhappiness to others and happiness to himself. I do not know of any rational ground for this view. ..."[ii] Morality and the ability to recognize it must come from somewhere. Given the fact that mankind universally recognizes morality and decency attests to something more than evolution. A much better explanation is that this ability comes from a source, because it does not appear to be intrinsic in all organisms. This explanation fits perfectly with the Bible, which states that mankind is created in the image of God (Genesis 1:26).

Is God a Delusion?

In his book *The God Delusion*, Oxford professor Richard Dawkins claims that religion in general—and Christianity in particular—is simply delusional. God is no more real than the tooth fairy, unicorns, or the Flying Spaghetti Monster. The Hebrew Bible is a book of Bronze Age myths and Jewish fairy tales. Jesus was just a regular Joe who ran afoul of the Roman authorities and got Himself crucified. The early Christians used Christianity to establish a political power base and exert control over others for their own benefit.

One of the main objections to belief in God is that intellectuals don't need these whimsical tales to live happy and successful lives. To an extent, that's true. There are plenty of happy, successful atheists. But there are also plenty of intelligent Christians who are just as successful. Just like atheists, there are Christians at every point on the intellectual spectrum.

What the militant variety of atheism refuses to admit is that Christians are discriminated against in academia. In some cases, Christians cannot pursue PhDs in the hard sciences, secure university teaching positions, or receive grant money because of their faith. One of the most stunning cases of discrimination was against Raymond Damadian, who invented the MRI. Two other scientists who continued his work were awarded the Nobel Prize, even though Damadian actually invented the machine. Although up to three recipients can be awarded the prize at one time, the inventor was totally shut out of any recognition for his contribution to the medical sciences. Rick Weiss, writing in the December 2003 issue of *Smithsonian* notes, "it is difficult not to at least consider … that scientists on the assembly or in other positions of influence could not abide Damadian's staunch support for 'creationist science.' "[iii]

A second objection to belief in God is that science has allegedly dispensed with the need for Him. This is especially troublesome because the scientific method cannot be used to detect evidence for God, yet it is cited as proof that He doesn't exist. Other evidence suggests that belief in God is rational and acceptable. The origin of the universe and the design and complexity that characterizes it must have an adequate explanation. The idea that order could come from disorder violates natural law, as does the idea that the universe could remain in a state of order despite the created order's unstoppable descent into a state of disorder. There remain many questions that doom current scientific explanations for a godless universe.

Third, Christianity is described as a virus. There is a great deal of eloquent talk about faith being a mental virus that can be killed by a vaccination of reason, meaning that children should be inoculated against Christianity at the earliest opportunity. There is a severe double standard at work here, however: many critics feel it is permissible to teach a child to be open-minded to all philosophies and worldviews except Christianity. Of course, there is no evidence that faith is a virus, and none is offered. It is simply a clever argument intended to ridicule. One could argue that atheism is a virus based on an equal lack of evidence.

In the end, it boils down to one of two options: (1) God exists and His existence can be implied through scientific means, or (2) God is a delusion in the minds of believers. We saw in chapter 2 that the universe had to have some kind of universally powerful, personal creator. The advances in science may not detect God directly, but they do show that something more than natural forces are at work. Three thousand years ago, pagans believed that the gods created the world from pre-existent material. Today we know that is not the case, but we also know that the universe cannot simply come from nowhere. The laws of science state that this universe had to be generated and could never have existed from time immemorial or else it would have run down by now. The more we know about science, the more we know that naturalistic explanations make less and less sense. Something—and someone—else is needed to satisfy our intellectual curiosity about the deep secrets of the universe in which we live.

First Things First

Some have claimed that God is a crutch for the weak who have a hard time coping with reality. The problem with claiming that God is simply a projection of a divine protector or cosmic parent is that this God makes moral and ethical demands of human beings that run counter to our nature. The very reason why some run from God is because they believe He is a cosmic dictator, carefully monitoring their every move and plotting their eternal doom should they commit the smallest infraction. People realize what kind of ethical demands being a Christian entails, and all too often they are afraid to take it on. The argument that God is a divine nanny really falls flat, with the reactions of millions militating against it.

Let's revisit Freud's argument for a moment. According to him and others, man just invented God to help him cope with life. The question that we have to ask is this: Why invent a God who makes

God Exists

stringent moral requirements, whose very presence is deadly and cannot be entered unless certain conditions are met (Exodus 33:20)? This would seem like an odd God to invent if a person merely wanted a cosmic enabler. It is strange to invent a God who punishes sin.

If the God of the Bible exists then there are many other considerations that come into play. It doesn't matter what our opinion on the existence of God is. Either He exists, or He doesn't. If we do believe in Him and He does not exist, then no amount of faith will create Him. If we don't believe in Him and He does exist, then no amount of disbelief will make Him go away.

Truth 4

The Bible is Historically Reliable

The Bible is both the most beloved and the most despised book ever written. More than one billion people in the world today look to the Bible as a reliable source of truth. They read it, cherish it, and use it as a guide for both behavior and belief. Others deride it as nothing more than an anthology of myths and legends. It goes without saying that the Christian faith stands or falls on the reliability of the Bible. Could this ancient book be historically reliable?

The stories of Old Testament heroes and New Testament miracle workers have led some to conclude that the Bible is little more than an epic saga, no more historical than the tales of ancient heroes and Greco-Roman gods. No one takes the stories of Hercules or Jason and the Argonauts seriously. Those stories have themes that are basic to the human condition—love and loss, tragedy and triumph. The Bible does, too.

In centuries past, people gave the Bible a great deal of respect. Today, the Bible is viewed, in the words of comedian Bill Maher, as "the book of Jewish fairy tales." If we could poll the American people, many would agree. In 2006, the Gallup News Service reported that only 28 percent of Americans believe that the Bible is the actual word of God.[i] But there is more to this issue than drive-by criticism. How do we classify the Bible? It contains a great deal of historical information, so do we consider it a history book? Yes and no. The Bible is not "history" as we understand it in the twenty-first century. But does it contain reliable historical information? Absolutely. All scholars, regardless of theological or religious orientation (or lack thereof) agree that at least parts of the Bible do contain kernels of genuine historical detail. But are there more than just a few nuggets of reliable information? That's the question.

Writing History

To begin our quest, we must first get a handle on what history *is*. There are two definitions of history: the actual events that took place at some point in the past, and the recording or recounting of those events by a historian. The first definition is objective. Either the events happened or they didn't. The second definition is much more subjective. In writing history, the historian is selective. Every author must determine which facts are important, and interpret those facts in light of the entire body of evidence pertaining to the person, place, or event about which he or she is writing. History is reconstructed by historians who, ideally, match their reconstructions as closely as possible to the events as they happened. In the end, however, every historian must make judgments, draw conclusions, and determine what evidence is relevant to the story being told.

As far as the Bible is concerned, is it historically accurate? Here we bring in our distinction between what happened and the recording of the events. Much of the Bible is not recorded in the genre of history. The works of the prophets and the poetic sections of Scripture are not history—they are prophetic and poetic literature. Neither are other portions of the Bible, such as the books of Leviticus and Deuteronomy, which fall under the category of law. Genesis chapters 1 and 2 make up a very small category called cosmology. This does not mean that the details recorded in these sections are fictional. It only means that those sections are not written in the form of history.

Several sections of Scripture preserve historical details, though they are not history. For instance, the Song of Moses in Exodus 15 is exactly that: a song. Yet it records the crossing of the Red Sea in Exodus 14. Another example is in Judges 5, referred to as the Song of Deborah. Judges 4 records the defeat of Jabin and his general Sisera in a narrative form. Judges 5 recounts the same episode in the form of a song. The same goes for the destruction of Jerusalem in the book of Lamentations. That book is, just as its title indicates, a particular form of poetic literature called a lamentation. There are many examples of lamentations from the ancient world, often recording military defeats. So we see that historical truth can be preserved in writing that does not fall into the genre of history.

While historians in the early part of the last century believed that objective history could be discovered (and many still do), some have veered off course toward a radical form of historical skepticism. A new breed of scholars has arisen who are known as "biblical minimalists." These scholars believe that the history recorded in the Bible existed only in the minds of the biblical authors and that "history" in the Bible should be distrusted unless there is independent confirmation of the events recorded. Archaeological evidence is held to be more important than written sources, because human writing contains beliefs, presuppositions, and biases that can distort the record of events. The minimalists are extreme skeptics when it comes to the biblical data, distrusting the record of any event unless outside evidence can be found to corroborate it.

The minimalist approach immediately raises a number of questions. What is the cause for this heightened skepticism? Why elevate other evidence, including other written documents, above the Bible? Does the Bible not qualify as evidence? How much proof is needed to verify any given event Scripture records? Why is the Bible held to a higher standard than other ancient works?

The minimalist camp operates on a level of skepticism that is far above the average person. Virtually no one insists on multiple avenues of verification for every new fact learned. If that were the case, no one would ever make it past the first article on the front page of the morning newspaper. There is a certain level of trust that the sources providing our information have done their jobs and sought to present the facts objectively. Newspapers can and do earn reputations for being too liberal or too conservative. Certain authors have reputations for slanting the information one way or another. Rarely do writers guilty of doing piecemeal work stay employed very long, because their work reflects upon their employer. In short, human writing can be identified, evaluated, and judged. The writing itself is the object of scrutiny, and the reader can determine for himself or herself whether that writing is factually accurate and objective or not. The same can be done with the Bible.

What Did the Biblical Authors Have in Mind?

An important question to ask is what were the biblical authors actually writing? Did they understand the modern concept of history? Some of the Bible, as we said above, is history, or at least history-like. Much of it is not, but again, that does not mean that the events recorded are fictional. History in the Bible is somewhat different than modern history. Historiography, the study of the writing of history, did not exist in biblical times. The first historian is generally considered to be the Greek author Herodotus (c. 484–c. 425 BC), the "father of history." Before that, history did not exist as a genre.

We often refer to Luke as a historian, which is generally accurate but needs to be explained. Luke was not a historian in the modern sense, but he did follow much the same procedure that modern historians employ in writing history. For instance, Luke 1:1-4 indicates that Luke was intensely concerned with obtaining eyewitness data for his biography of Jesus. Modern historians frequently refer to written sources, while Luke and other writers in antiquity relied upon what they called "the living voice." Historians in the ancient world prized eyewitness accounts over written records, in part because a living witness may communicate much more information than a piece of paper through things like the inflection of the voice, expressions, and accompanying gestures. For instance, a gifted storyteller engages his audience and may provide details that simply cannot be captured in writing.

Relying on living testimony does not imply that the frailty of human memory contributed to an inferior product of writing. In fact, it is very nearly the opposite. The educated elite prized the use of memory and looked with disdain on those who relied on written records. To paraphrase the Greek philosopher Socrates, "The greatest philosophy is never written down." Writing was viewed as cheating. Anyone could learn to read, but not everyone was equipped with the mental faculties to remember vast amounts of information.

We must be careful not to read modern custom back into the past. In an oral culture, people had much better ability to remember things than moderns do today. We live in a culture unaccustomed to the need to remember everything. We have sticky notes, calendars, day planners, and PDA's to remember everything for us. Because most people are literate, we simply jot down a quick note for future reference and often forget about whatever it was until that note jogs our memories. People in the ancient world had no such luxury, so memory was vital. Even when one studies the Gospels, as much as 80-90 percent of Jesus' words had a poetic ring to them, making them easier to remember for His listeners. As the great teacher, Jesus made it easy for His audiences to remember what He taught.

Modern skeptics frequently attempt to hold the Bible to the same standards one might expect of modern historiography. It is thoroughly unfair, however, to expect authors from a different culture and mindset two thousand years ago to write according to standards from the twenty-first-century Western world. The biblical authors should be judged by the same standards as other ancient writers, who often used literary techniques in their works that do not have modern correspondents. This includes the following:

Hyperbole. Solomon is described as being so wealthy that silver is as abundant as stone (2 Chronicles 1:15). However, when we compare the king's actual wealth with other ancient Near Eastern kings, Solomon's wealth is fairly pedestrian. Exaggeration is something everyone uses, whether it's describing something that "weighs a ton" or saying "I'm so hungry I could eat a horse." The biblical authors were no different.

Abbreviation. Time is sometimes condensed in Scripture. After his failed siege of Jerusalem, Sennacherib goes back home, where he is murdered by his two sons in a *coup d'état* (Isaiah 37:37, 38). According to Assyrian records, he wasn't killed for another twenty years, but the way the biblical author wrote it appears that his sons killed him immediately upon his return. While modern readers may raise an eyebrow, there would have been no confusion with the original audience familiar with the events that took place.

Non-literal use of numbers. Not everyone in the ancient world used numbers with modern scientific accuracy. For instance, the number forty often stood for "one generation," which is how this seems to appear in places like Judges when describing some of the lengths of the judges' reigns. The same is true for extrabiblical writings. On a victory monument, King Mesha of Moab records that Israel had oppressed his county for forty years, while the figure is actually closer to twenty-two. The difference is easily explained by the fact that Mesha referred to the period of time using a representative number, while the biblical author used a literal one.

Lack of rigid chronology. Of all the Gospels, Luke has the best claim to being arranged chronologically. This does not mean that the other Gospels are inaccurate or untrustworthy. It simply means that the biographers of Jesus arranged their material in different ways to communicate their messages. This may sound strange to modern readers but was done frequently in the ancient world. The point is that we need to judge the Bible by the standards of the period in which it was written, not force modern standards onto the ancient authors who had no way of knowing how things would be written two millennia later.

While many of the differences between the biblical writers should be noted, it is also important to note that they share similarities with modern historians. The ancient writers often chose to leave out less-important details or emphasize other events they considered relevant to their message. Sometimes the writers de-emphasized things. For instance, Omri is mentioned in only a handful of verses in 1 Kings 16, leaving the impression that he was a minor king. In reality, he was one of the most powerful in the history of the Northern Kingdom. Why did the biblical author give him such short shrift? Simple: God isn't impressed with the accomplishments of evil men, and neither are His authors.

Holy Myth

I remember watching *The Clash of the Titans* as a boy. Every year it seemed the movie came on sometime during the holiday season, and I watched it from start to finish each time. I loved watching Perseus interact with the Greek gods, tame the noble Pegasus, and battle fantastic monsters. Later I studied the Greek myths in middle school, struck by the creative genius of the ancients in inventing monsters like the sphinx, the gorgons, and the kraken. For me, the Bible was always very different from the fanciful epics of the Greeks.

It wasn't until I was in college that I came across accusations that the Bible was no more real than the Greek myths I read about in middle school. I was in a senior seminar studying ancient Near Eastern history when I came into contact with scholars who confidently declared the Bible to be nothing more than ancient fiction. Even on the popular level, critics frequently refer to the Bible as a book of fairy tales and Bronze Age myths. How do we tell the difference between truth and fiction?

It's important to look back at the myths of the Greeks and Romans, Egyptians, and Babylonians. They are filled with fantastic monsters, heroes who are larger than life, and epic struggles with cosmic implications. These are the mainstays of ancient mythology. But where are they to be found in the Bible? That's quite a different story.

If the Bible were nothing more than a literary creation invented from whole cloth, one would expect there to be a great deal of difference between the Bible and extrabiblical records. A fictional story written by someone unable to carefully research the life and times about which he is writing will not mention particular details in his fiction. He would know that discrepancies could reveal the true character of his work. Rather than finding such discrepancies between the Bible and secular history, we find a great deal of agreement between the two. The Old Testament is particularly susceptible to the charges of being nothing more than Near Eastern mythology, yet we find remarkable agreement between the Bible and the ancient evidence.

The Bible's accuracy can be seen in part in the work of Luke. Archaeologist Sir William Ramsay (1851-1939) studied under liberal German scholarship at the famous University of Tubingen and approached the notion that Luke was an accurate historian with a degree of hostility. He says

> I began with a mind unfavorable to [Acts] … but more recently I found myself often brought into contact with the Book of Acts as an authority for the topography, antiquities, and society of Asia Minor. It was gradually borne in upon me that in various details the narrative showed marvelous truth."[ii]

Paul told Timothy that false teachers would come into the church attempting to pass off myths and fables as truth (2 Timothy 4:3, 4). This was as true in the ancient world as it is today. Modern myths include the teaching of Scientology. Its founder, science fiction author L. Ron Hubbard, invented a religion in which a race of beings called

Thetans used evolution to create human beings. The Thetans became nothing more than disembodied spirits when a nuclear explosion destroyed all life on earth seventy-four trillion years ago. But Hubbard is not alone in his foray into religious belief. Several other modern religious systems are the result of the fertile human imagination.

Ancient writers also expanded on the biblical accounts. In the rabbinic literature, we find stories such as the legend of Lilith, supposedly the first created woman. She did not submit to Adam and fled from Eden. After God created Eve, Adam returned to Lilith (who bore him a number of children that later became demons) before eventually settling down with wife number two. According to legend, Lilith became a demonic queen who was known for murdering infants and young boys. Modern vampire tales sometimes trace their origin to Adam's fictional first wife.

In the end, we see that religions of human creation are often fanciful and extravagant. We don't find in Scripture the descriptive extravagance to which other ancient writers were prone. There is virtually no attempt made by mythology to ground itself in actual history, unlike the Bible. It is written very soberly, and should not be presumed guilty by association.

What About All Those Errors?

A friend of mine stopped by a fast food restaurant for a quick bite to eat. The cashier wore a simple necklace with a gold cross. He smiled and struck up a conversation, asking about her faith. She answered, "I'm Jewish, but I believe that Jesus is the Messiah." They chatted for a while, and my friend happily went on his way.

Two weeks later my friend visited the restaurant again. He saw the same cashier, except instead of a golden cross, she wore a Star of David around her neck. He asked her what had changed. She replied, "I found a passage where Jesus quotes the book of Zechariah, but says that it comes from Jeremiah. If Jesus made a mistake like that, he couldn't be the Messiah. So now I'm back to being Jewish." (In Matthew 27:9, 10, Jesus refers to the major and minor prophets collectively as the "book of Jeremiah" after its largest book, just as He refers to the poetic books as the "Psalms" in Luke 24:44.)

It is often alleged from the common critic all the way to the accomplished scholar that the Bible is full of errors, discrepancies, and contradictions. Many Christians believe in the inerrancy of the Bible, which states that the Bible is true in all that it teaches regardless of the subject. This means that the Bible is true not only on all matters of doctrine and ethics but is equally true in matters concerning social, physical, and life sciences.

The internal claims of Scripture say that the Bible is inspired (better, "exhaled") by God (2 Timothy 3:16). It also notes that it is the product of divine guidance where the human authors are concerned (2 Peter 1:21). While the Bible was written by human hands, it was also written under the oversight of God. Because He cannot lie (1 Samuel 15:29; Hebrews 6:18), it should also go without saying that He would not misrepresent the truth or allow His authors to do so, either.

There are three important indications of the Bible's inerrancy. The first is historical. From what we currently understand from ancient history, we do not find contradictions. This makes natural sense, since the authors were often recording events as they experienced them in their historical contexts. We do find some books being written after the events, such as Judges or Chronicles, but many of the authors took part in the events they recorded.

The second indication is scientific. Science has yet to prove a scientific error in Scripture. This is due, in part, to the fact that there is a great deal of phenomenological language in the Bible, a description of reality from the perspective of the viewer. Critics often claim that the Bible has a geocentric view of the universe, supported by the fact that the medieval church argued the same using Scripture. Yet even today we still refer to the sunrise and sunset, understanding that the sun only appears to rise and set from our frame of reference. In truth, the church was defending a viewpoint promoted by medieval scientists.

The third indication is prophetic. We find biblical authors speaking of events years before they happen. One particularly noteworthy example is Ezekiel 26, which describes the destruction of the Phoenician city of Tyre centuries before it took place. The prophet says that the rock upon which the city stood would be scraped bare and fishermen would use it as a place to repair their nets (vv.4, 5). Alexander the Great did exactly that in 332 BC, throwing the rubble from the ruined city into the Mediterranean. Today, local fishermen use the place as a spot to repair their fishing nets, just as the prophet claimed.

Are there legitimate difficulties in the Bible? Of course, but they are few and far between. Actually, there are several logical reasons why a passage may be particularly difficult. First, it may be due to a scribal error. There are a number of scribal errors in the text of the Bible. But does this mean the Bible is untrustworthy? Not at all. It merely means that at some point in the ancient past, a copyist made a slip of the pen. Due to the hundreds and thousands of manuscripts in our possession, errors are easily detected in comparing manuscripts with one another. A copyist's error does not invalidate the work of the original, inspired author. Another reason for supposed Bible contradictions is misinterpretation on the part of the reader. Critical websites all across the Internet challenge the Bible, yet overwhelmingly the majority of this material is based on the reader's failure to understand the Bible and the cultural context in which it was written. As our understanding of the Bible and the original languages in which it was written expands, these problems are becoming fewer and fewer.

Look Before You Leap

The Bible is a remarkably accurate book. Christians may be confident that the so-called problems—of which critics seem to find a virtually endless supply—are often explained by the fact that critics fail to understand what the Bible is saying. This is especially true for sources on the Internet (otherwise known as the World Wide Rumor Mill), although it is also found among the ranks of academia. Evidence from the ancient world is very often fragmentary, which requires scholars to make informed interpretations and educated guesses. Scholars often disagree with one another, and it is a constant possibility that scholars criticizing the Bible are flatly wrong, despite whatever impressive credentials they may possess.

We could fill many more pages of examples of biblical critics who laid charges at the Bible's feet, only to later be corrected by the progress of knowledge. As increasing amounts of evidence come to light, believers may have an equally increasing amount of trust in the reliability of the Bible. Scholars are continually making new discoveries in various fields that have a bearing on Scripture. One of these areas is archaeology, a subject addressed in chapter 5.

Truth 5

Archaeology Confirms the Bible's Reliability

Whenever I mention the word "archaeology" the first things that come to people's minds are (1) Indiana Jones, (2) buried treasure, and (3) exotic locations, often in that order. Something of all three is involved in archaeology today, although not as much in times past. Europeans exploring the relatively wild Middle East in the eighteenth and nineteenth centuries did experience high adventure on occasion. At that time, archaeology was little more than unsophisticated treasure hunting. Wealthy elites traveled to the Middle East, reclining under lace umbrellas, sipping tea from fine china as hired hands did the manual labor. You won't find any of that today!

Archaeology has unearthed a number of wonderful treasures from the ancient world. From the stunning relics inside the tomb of Tutankhamun to the inlaid skulls of the Incas, museums proudly display the most important finds that archaeology has uncovered. Unfortunately, TV producers know that sensationalism sells, so documentaries often highlight the high profile discoveries and depict their foray into the past as a grand adventure. Documentaries about monumental architecture or ancient pottery wouldn't do very well in the ratings. Viewing audiences want to see treasure and lots of it.

The last few centuries have been particularly tough on the Bible. The rise of various types of criticism has undermined faith in the reliability of the text and caused even solid Christians to question God's Word. Viewing the Bible with abject skepticism is now seen as the intelligent thing to do. Critics claim, "Everyone knows that intelligent people don't take the Bible literally." Well, what if we just take it at face value?

One of the areas of scholarship that has consistently heated up in the last few decades is the discipline of biblical archaeology. Archaeology began with ministers who traveled to the Holy Land with a spade in one hand and a Bible in the other. As the field has become increasingly specialized, many scholars have rejected the idea that archaeology could provide substantial information to corroborate the Bible. Some would argue that recent discoveries undermine the Bible's reliability.

Archaeology and the Old Testament

Scholarship has been highly critical of the Bible quite often. Beginning in earnest in the eighteenth century, critics argued that the Old Testament, particularly the Pentateuch, was a piecemeal collection of different documents that were edited together very late in Jewish history. They denied the authorship of Moses and declared the patriarchal narratives a literary fiction. The Bible, in short, was uninspired by any higher power.

In the late nineteenth century and early twentieth century, critics said that Moses could not have written the Pentateuch because writing did not exist when he lived. We now know that writing goes back at least as far as 3300 BC. Critics also said that the biblical authors invented Sargon II (722-705 BC), known to us from Isaiah 20:1. In 1843, archaeologist Paul-Émile Botta found his palace at Khorsabad (called Dur-Sharrukin in ancient times, literally translated as "Fortress of Sargon"). Critics also said that the biblical writers invented the Hittites, whose capital city Hattuša was discovered near modern day Boğazkale. While these discoveries vindicated the Bible a century ago, what about more recent times?

Progress in our understanding of the ancient world inevitably brings new challenges to studying the Bible. Older theories are replaced by newer ones. Newer theories are contested in different circles. Some say that archaeology proves the Bible, others that it disproves God's Word. With all of this disagreement, we are tempted to ask, "Is there anything we can know for sure?"

Archaeology has been particularly helpful in bringing biblical characters to life. David and Solomon are some of the most maligned figures in Scripture, frequently claimed to be nothing more than myth or legend and consigned to the same category as Arthur and his court at Camelot. Evidence from recent discoveries show that David and Solomon ruled an impressive kingdom. David is referred to in two victory monuments called the Tel Dan Inscription and the Mesha Stele. The inscriptions on these monuments refer to the Southern Kingdom as the "house of David." "The house of X" was a common way of referring to a kingdom by using the name of a historical ruler, so it seems that ancient sources did indeed consider David to be a real person.

Unlike that of his father, Solomon's name has eluded discovery. This is not surprising because Jerusalem has been destroyed and rebuilt more than a dozen times, and a modern city sits directly on top of the ancient one preventing extensive excavation. While his supposedly wealthy kingdom is laughed at as a mythical creation, an Egyptian source provides hard evidence of the kingdom's existence and its impressive economic status.

Pharaoh Shishak I invaded Palestine in c. 925 BC, during the reign of Rehoboam, Solomon's son (c. 932-915 BC). The pharaoh looted a number of cities in a brief military campaign but died shortly after he returned home. Pharaohs customarily donated plunder from their campaigns to the Egyptian temples upon their return from war. Because Shishak had not been able to do so prior to his death, his son Osorkon I donated the wealth in his father's stead. It was the single largest donation in the history of ancient Egypt, roughly 383 tons of gold and silver. How does a mythical kingdom accumulate hundreds of millions—perhaps even several billions—of dollars worth of precious metals?

Numerous discoveries have validated other characters in the Bible, from extrabiblical characters mentioned in Scripture to biblical figures whose existence has been unfairly questioned. Foreign kings mentioned in the Bible, such as Sargon (Isaiah 20:1) and Belshazzar (Daniel 5:1) are now well-known in extrabiblical sources. Even minor characters such as Sanballat (governor of Samaria), Tobiah, Geshem (Nehemiah 2:19), and perhaps even Balaam (Numbers 22-24) are known from archaeological discoveries. Nearly every king in the Divided Monarchy is mentioned in Assyrian and Babylonian records.

Sometimes archaeology comes up short. In the case of the patriarchs, archaeologists have never found direct evidence that they existed. This is not surprising, since Abraham and his family were nomads. They moved often and never left anything behind that would survive as a lasting testimony to their presence. Archaeology has unearthed a great deal of corroborating evidence, however. The events, customs, names, and legal documents of the patriarchal narratives fit what we know of the ancient Near East in the early second millennium. While we do not have direct evidence of their existence, there is more than enough indirect evidence to place the burden of proof on the skeptic who denies their existence.

In the case of Joseph, there is no doubt that someone with direct familiarity with Egypt wrote the story. Moses probably wrote down the oral traditions passed down to him while the Hebrews were living in Egypt. What we do know is that the story rings true. The twenty shekel price tag for Joseph (Genesis 37:28), the seventy days needed for mummification and subsequent mourning (50:3), and the fact that non-Egyptians like Joseph could be viziers are just part of the biblical evidence drawn from ancient Egypt. Critics say that these stories were invented centuries later, but there's a key problem with that assertion: Hebrew scribes did not have access to research libraries or ancient records. They had no way of finding out the historical details needed to compose a convincing piece of historical fiction. It would be like someone today writing a story about Charlemagne, and by chance getting even the smallest details correct despite not knowing anything about his life, his times, or the language he spoke.

Archaeology and the New Testament

As with the Old Testament, archaeology has helped locate some of the characters of the New Testament in real time and space. Pontius Pilate was at one time considered a fictive person, but we now know from historical sources that he was a real person. Archaeologists even found his name in an inscription. Excavating in a theater in Caesarea Maritama in 1961, excavators turned up a stone with an inscription bearing the title "Pontius Pilatus, Prefect of Judea."

Other inscriptions mention minor characters in the New Testament. Gallio, proconsul of Achaia (Acts 18:12-17) is mentioned in an inscription at Delphi. Lysanias, tetrarch of Abilene (Luke 3:1) is probably referred to in an inscription mentioning a temple dedication. The name of Paul's friend Erastus (Acts 19:22) has almost certainly been found in Corinth in a dedicatory inscription. Sergius Paulus, the first convert on Cyprus, was also proconsul during the time Paul visited the island (13:7). In 1877 archaeologists found an inscription bearing Sergius Paulus' name near Paphos, corroborating the New Testament text.

Friends of the apostles aren't the only ones turning up in the archaeological record. Joseph Caiaphas, high priest at the time Jesus was crucified, surfaced in 1990. His ossuary (bone-box) was discovered by chance in Jerusalem. The inscription on the ossuary mentions "Joseph, son of Caiaphas," whose name is also mentioned by the historian Josephus. He makes a brief appearance in John's Gospel (11:49-53).

Playing in the Dirt

Archaeology is a fascinating discipline that has discovered a number of things that impact how Christians view the Bible. It must be noted, however, that archaeology cannot "prove" the Bible. Unfortunately, many Christians assume that archaeology can prove the inspiration of Scripture. It is not designed to do that, and can at best only offer circumstantial evidence (we'll look at inspiration in greater detail in chapter 9). That does not mean that archaeology is useless, only limited. A better way to think about it is that archaeology illuminates, supplements, or corroborates the Bible, all of which are very valuable in their own rights.

We must also realize that an inescapable part of the archaeological enterprise is the fact that scholars all begin with presuppositions or preconceptions. Part of the "proof" that critics look for archaeology to provide isn't necessarily the kind of proof that can be offered through material evidence. In some cases, the material evidence may be lacking entirely.

The astronomer Carl Sagan once remarked, "The absence of evidence is not the evidence of absence." Given the fragmentary nature of the archaeological record, this is the truth. Just because current evidence of something may be lacking doesn't mean that it never existed. It just means that it didn't leave any evidence of its existence. Any traces could easily be wiped away by a number of environmental factors. We can think of several "fractions" that greatly limit the amount of information that archaeology can provide for us:

Only a fraction of the evidence was buried. Not everything survived to be buried in the first place. When we think of the fact that no inscriptions from David and Solomon have been uncovered, one plausible explanation is that later, hostile monarchs destroyed monuments from previous rulers (after all, the monarchy had a lot of bad apples). Another possibility is that inscriptions left behind may have been reused, which happened quite a bit in the ancient world. Furthermore, not all evidence makes it into the archaeological record. Things that are perishable will obviously deteriorate to some extent before specialists can uncover it. Even artifacts housed in carefully controlled environments in the world's best museums are slowly deteriorating at this very moment. No matter how hard we try, we simply cannot stop the march of time.

Only a fraction of the ancient sites will be excavated. Not every ancient site can be excavated. Practical concerns determine where archaeologists can excavate. If water, food, shelter, and electricity are not readily available at a prospective location, chances are it won't be excavated. Adverse political conditions also impact excavations. Some places in the modern Middle East are off limits because of the threat of violence.

Only a fraction of an ancient site will be excavated. No archaeologist exhaustively excavates any particular site. Excavation costs a lot of money, so when archaeologists think they have a handle on the most important information, they move on to the publication phase to report their findings. Excavation can also be very slow work, so years of work may only uncover a limited portion of any given site.

Only a fraction of the discoveries will be published and reported. Not everything that happens on a dig will be reported. In some cases, archaeologists may do a very poor job of reporting, or not report at all (thankfully, those cases are very rare).

The fragmentary nature of archaeology is both helpful and unhelpful to the Christian faith. Notice that I did not say helpful and harmful. While archaeology can locate people and places in antiquity and provide hard evidence that attests the reality of much of what is mentioned in the Bible, it will not always be so. The picture archaeology paints will be somewhat incomplete, and not everything that existed from the ancient world will have survived to be discovered by modern experts. Many discoveries say nothing about the Bible, but no discoveries have overturned the Bible. As the Jewish scholar Nelson Glueck once famously remarked, "It may be stated categorically that no archaeological discovery has ever controverted a biblical reference."[i]

Sadly, archaeology is sometimes misused by popular Christian apologists. Individuals may use archaeological evidence as a proof of the Bible's divine inspiration. Archaeology is not capable of doing that, at least not directly. While it can do a great many things, such as determine when an event occurred or what kind of culture existed in a particular area, it cannot prove that God spoke to the prophets or that the Holy Spirit superintended the writing and compilation of the Bible. Archaeology is concerned with examining the physical remains left behind by ancient cultures, and that evidence simply doesn't overtly speak to inspiration. Again, that isn't to say that archaeology is useless. In fact, it is quite useful when used properly. When used correctly, is speaks indirectly to inspiration as it corroborates the events recorded in Scripture.

How Much Evidence Do You Need?

The problem with the archaeological record is that definitive proof is not often easily had. Critics frequently make demands for proof that exceed the available evidence, and sometimes violate common sense. I remember running across a website where an atheist posted a challenge to believers. In a very magnanimous gesture, he confessed that if Christians could supply proof of the existence of God and of the Bible's reliability, he would change his mind and become a believer. He offered a list of suggested proofs that approached the absurd. He asked for believers to show him whether God had encoded the cure for cancer somewhere in the pages of Scripture and challenged Christians to show him proof of extraterrestrial life that believed in Jesus. His "open-minded" request was for the impossible and probably wasn't even genuine in the first place.

We might think of various pieces of ancient evidence that serve as anchors holding the Bible firmly in human history. Here is a quick list of a few more discoveries that anchor the Bible's place in history:

Beni Hasan Tomb Painting. In an Egyptian tomb dating to the nineteenth to twentieth centuries BC, this tomb painting shows Canaanites traveling freely into Egypt, the same situation found in Genesis with respect to the patriarchs (Genesis 12:10). Since the Egyptian borders closed to outsiders around 1650 BC, then the patriarchs must have lived prior to that time. While some scholars believe that the stories of the patriarchs are fiction, this evidence demonstrates that an authentic story must predate 1650 BC, just as the Bible depicts.

The Black Obelisk of Shalmaneser. Found in a royal palace at Nimrud in 1846, this monument depicts either King Jehu or his servant bowing down and bringing tribute to the Assyrian monarch in the eighth century BC (cf. 2 Kings 9-10). This is just one of dozens of references to biblical kings in Assyrian and Babylonian records.

Sennacherib's Prism. This six-sided clay prism records the invasion of Judah by the Assyrian King Sennacherib in 701 BC. He boasts that his forces had Hezekiah trapped in Jerusalem "like a bird in a cage." If Sennacherib had conquered the city, he would have done what all ancient kings did: glory in the devastation of his enemies. Since the prism mentions nothing of the conquest of the city, it is obvious that Sennacherib failed to conquer it, just as 2 Chronicles 32 and Isaiah 36-37 indicate.

Siloam Tunnel Inscription. Discovered in 1880, this inscription tells the story of the completion of a water tunnel commissioned by Hezekiah to bring water to Jerusalem during times of war (cf. 2 Kings. 20:20; 2 Chronicles 32:30). The handwriting style of the inscription dates to the time of Hezekiah as well.

Ketef Hinnom Inscription. Thanks to a chance discovery in 1979, archaeologists discovered two small silver amulets bearing the prayer from Numbers 6:24-26. Dating to the seventh century BC, these tiny scrolls contain the earliest example of a biblical text found to date.

Cyrus' Cylinder. This small, barrel-shaped cylinder records the decree of Cyrus to allow people captured by the Babylonians to return to their native homelands. Although the Jews are not mentioned explicitly, the cylinder fits with Cyrus' policies toward foreigners (cf. 2 Chronicles 36:23).

The Alexamenos Graffito. Discovered in 1856, this piece of graffiti (second to third century AD) on the plaster wall of a Roman guardhouse shows a man worshiping a crucified figure. The inscription reads, "Alexamenos worships his god." It is clear that the crucified figure is none other than Christ, since He is the only crucified deity in antiquity. This shows that even the "man on the street" knew that Christians worshiped a crucified God, contrary to the claims of some modern authors who teach that the Christians invented a deified Christ in the fourth century or later.

The Meggido Church Inscription. Like the Alexamenos Graffito, this inscription, which mentions "God Jesus Christ," provides tangible proof that Christians believed in a divine Christ as early as the third century AD, only about two centuries after Christ was crucified. Found in the mid-1990s, the church is one of the earliest ever discovered.

Conclusion

The history of biblical studies has its fair share of scholars who became increasingly confident in the Bible's reliability after investigating the archaeological evidence. As we saw in the last chapter, Sir William Ramsay set out to disprove the books of Luke and Acts as reliable sources, and managed to convince himself that Luke was not only correct but concluded Luke was "a historian of the first rank."[ii] William Foxwell Albright, professor of Semitic Languages at the Johns Hopkins University from 1929-1958, is generally viewed as one of the greatest archaeologists of the twentieth century. He began as a skeptic, but, like Ramsay, he investigated the archaeological evidence and concluded that the biblical record was trustworthy. His opinion is shared by a number of modern scholars as well. He said, "There can be no doubt that archeology has confirmed the substantial historicity of the Old Testament tradition."[iii]

The Christian must be careful in examining the evidence, not because it goes against the Bible, but because some critics will

Archaeology Confirms the Bible's Reliability

distort it in order to make the Bible appear less reliable. Unfortunate though it may be, some scholars can and do pursue personal agendas with the evidence. Scholars such as these are in the minority, however. Even those who do not believe in the inspiration of Scripture frequently have no problem affirming the reality of many of the individuals and events the Bible mentions.

The amassing evidence from the archaeological record is continuing to prove that the Bible can be trusted and that the events it records can often be located in actual history. While one must be careful to handle the evidence properly, there is little doubt that appropriate use of archaeology increasingly shows that the stories of the Bible are rooted in historical reality. That isn't surprising, since the biblical writers clearly expected their work to be viewed as relating to real people and events.

Truth 6

Jesus Really Lived

Jesus is one of the best-known figures in the world. Even after two thousand years, He makes the headlines with unsurpassed regularity. We see Him splashed across the covers of magazines at Christmas and Easter and again in tabloids offering New Year's prophecies and predictions at the local supermarket. The date of His birth is used as a benchmark for history, and He has dominated Western civilization ever since. Regardless of time, place, or culture, no other figure in history has the perpetual popularity that Jesus enjoys.

In 2006, *USA Today* carried a story about an Italian atheist who sued a priest for claiming that Jesus really lived and was born in Bethlehem. In Viterbo, Italy (25 miles northwest of Rome), Luigi Cascioli sued Reverend Enrico Righi, a parish priest. Citing an Italian anti-fraud law, Cascioli claimed that Righi's parish profited from the "fable of Christ's life" and that the Gospels are filled with contradictions. The judge later dismissed the suit. Cascioli was then fined by an appeals court in Rome for bringing a fraudulent suit, but he vows never to pay the $1,900 judgment against him.[i] The incident brings up a vital question that every human being must answer: Did Jesus really live on earth?

Audiences at the turn of the twenty-first century have been bombarded with information about Jesus. Unfortunately, much of it comes from TV documentaries that frequently interview skeptical scholars; the few believers that are allowed brief snippets of interview time are made to sound like irrational fundamentalists.

Critics routinely approach the Bible with radical skepticism. While other ancient books are innocent until proven guilty, the opposite is true when the Bible is examined. Because this is the case, the ancient evidence becomes incredibly important in corroborating the claims made by Scripture.

The Ancient Voices Speak

Simon Greenleaf was a lawyer highly respected on both sides of the Atlantic. He said, "Every document apparently ancient, coming from the proper repository or custody, and bearing on its face no evident marks of forgery, the law presumes to be genuine and devolves on the opposing party the burden of proving it to be otherwise."[ii] This is the approach routinely taken by the vast majority of scholars who examine ancient texts, regardless of time or culture. There is really only one exception to this rule: the Bible.

Many can and do accuse the early Christians of fabricating stories about Jesus, if not inventing Him out of whole cloth altogether. As many critics have said, "The Bible would never be permitted the court of evidence. It's biased. It is theologically-driven and was never intended as history. The early Christians wrote what would best benefit them and expand their power base." Christians needed a figure like this to rally around, some argue. The early Christians were pushing an agenda. So what do other sources say? Would objective writers confirm or deny the claims made by the New Testament authors?

The Gospels are supported by a number of ancient writers who mention Christ. There are additional writers who refer to Christ without mentioning Him by name, but we'll stick to the ones that scholars generally agree refer to Jesus. We can divide the early witnesses that mention Jesus into the two broad categories of Roman and Jewish sources, although there are many more that reference Christ indirectly. We will focus on those that mention Him explicitly.

The Roman Sources. In his works, Cornelius Tacitus (c. AD 55-120) has one mention of Jesus and two of Christianity. In his work *Annals*, written c. AD 115, he says

> Nero ... inflicted the most exquisite tortures on a class hated for their abominations, called Christians by the populace. Christus, from whom the name had its origin, suffered the extreme penalty during the reign of Tiberius at the hands of one of our procurators, Pontius Pilatus, and a most mischievous superstition, thus checked for the moment, again broke out not only in Judea, the first source of the evil, but even in Rome ....[iii]

As one of the most important historians in Rome and a first century witness, his mention of Jesus is vitally important. He affirms a great deal about the Christian faith, including its birth in Jerusalem, which served as something of a headquarters of the fledgling movement. He also mentions the fact that it quickly migrated to Rome, where the church was quite strong early on. Some have suggested that the fact that Christianity broke out again may be an indirect reference to the resurgence of the church after Christ's resurrection.[iv] Jesus was popular during His life, but the Bible is clear that after the crucifixion His disciples are disillusioned and forlorn. When He appears to them, their faith is once again enflamed and they turn into crusading apostles. The second breaking out may refer to this secondary movement.

The Roman historian Gaius Suetonius Tranquillas, about whom little is known, mentions Jesus in his biographical material concerning Emperor Claudius (AD 41-54). He says, "Because the Jews at Rome caused continuous disturbances at the instigation of Chrestus, he expelled them from the city."ᵛ Who is Chrestus? It appears to be a Latinized form of Christ, or the Greek *Christos* (it is very similar to the spelling Tacitus uses for Christ). The interesting part of this brief mention is that in AD 49, Claudius expelled a number of Jews from Rome because of riots that took place. Note that in Acts 18:2, Paul meets a Jewish couple named Aquila and Priscilla, who had recently left Italy.

The Roman governor Pliny the Younger served as governor of the Roman province of Bithynia in modern-day Asia Minor. Some of his correspondence dating to c. AD 112 mentions the Christians. The governor decided to take action against the Christians but first asked for advice from Emperor Trajan. Of the Christians he says

> They were in the habit of meeting on a certain fixed day before it was light, when they sang in alternate verses a hymn to Christ, as to a god, and bound themselves by a solemn oath, not to any wicked deeds, but never to commit any fraud, theft, or adultery, never to falsify their word, nor deny a trust when they should be called upon to deliver it up.ᵛⁱ

Though they appeared to be model citizens, Pliny persecuted the Christians and forced any whom he arrested to disavow Christ or else be executed. The Romans were highly suspicious of secretive groups, and Christians seemed to have compounded the problem by being so popular in Pliny's province that the temples were all but deserted. Pliny wanted to get rid of this heretical movement as he saw it, and Trajan largely commended his efforts. In a letter from the emperor, Pliny was told to carry through with his actions, but to refrain from searching for Christians or from accepting anonymous testimony against them.

The Jewish Sources. The Jewish general and historian Flavius Josephus (c. AD 37-97) is yet another in our line-up of first century non-Christian witnesses to Jesus. He has two brief references to Christ, the shorter of which refers to James as "the brother of Jesus."[vii] The longer reference, called the *Testimonium Flavianum*, is where Josephus tells something about Christ:

> Now there was about this time Jesus, a wise man, *if it be lawful to call him a man,* for he was a doer of wonderful works, a teacher of such men as receive the truth with pleasure. He drew over to him both many of the Jews and many of the Gentiles. *He was [the] Christ.* And when Pilate, at the suggestion of the principal men amongst us, had condemned him to the cross, those that loved him at the first did not forsake him, *for he appeared to them alive again the third day; as the divine prophets had foretold these and ten thousand other wonderful things concerning him.* And the tribe of Christians, so named from him, are not extinct at this day."[viii] (italics added)

The mention of Jesus here is hotly debated, and critics are quite fond of claiming that this material is fraudulent and was inserted by Christians to legitimize Jesus. The difficulty is that some of what Josephus says could not have been written by a Jew (set off in italics in the quotation cited previously). For instance, Josephus would not have called Him the Christ. It is perhaps the result of a well-meaning Christian who inserted explanatory material. Still, most of what Josephus says is not questioned by scholars. Except for the obvious Christian references, the rest is virtually unchallenged by historians. Wayne House notes that prominent scholars of Josephus today have argued that the bulk of the passage referring to Jesus is absolutely authentic, citing one authority who says the passage is "accepted as authentic by almost all scholars."[ix] This stands in stark contrast to critics who claim that scholars see the entire passage as a forgery.

In an Arabic translation dating to the tenth century, the wording is a bit more cautious. It deletes the phrases "if it be lawful to call him a man" and "He was [the] Christ." It also adds that the resurrection was merely "reported." Despite the three additions, most of what Josephus says is attested as genuine. This is a far cry from the "fraudulent text" alleged by the average critic. Noted New Testament scholar James Charlesworth said, "We can now be as certain as historical research will presently allow that Josephus did refer to Jesus."[x]

The Babylonian Talmud mentions Jesus' crucifixion (*Sanhedrin* 43a). Many, perhaps most, scholars believe this is a solid reference to Jesus. It dates somewhere between the late first and late second century, but also refers to Jesus by His Jewish name:

> On the eve of the Passover Yeshu was hanged. For forty days before the execution took place, a herald went forth and cried, "He is going forth to be stoned because he has practiced sorcery and enticed Israel to apostasy. Any one who can say anything in his favour, let him come forward and plead on his behalf." But since nothing was brought forward in his favor, he was hanged on the eve of the Passover.

The term "hanged" is sometimes used as a synonym for crucifixion (Luke 23:39; Galatians 3:13). Stoning is the prescribed punishment for blasphemy, which is the offense of which Jesus is charged (Leviticus 24:16). Instead, it appears Roman involvement dictated crucifixion. The forty days of heralding is not mentioned in the New Testament, although it was common Jewish practice.[xi] It may be that the later Jewish writer inserted this detail.

One final note is to be found in the works of a historian named Thallus. His history of the Eastern Mediterranean is now lost, but there is a reference preserved in the writings of Julius Africanus (c. AD 221). In his work *Chronography*, Africanus mentions that Thallus recorded a cosmic event, including a violent earthquake (cf. Matthew 27:51) and great darkness (cf. Luke 23:44) in Judea during the Passover season. Thallus called it a solar eclipse, but an eclipse cannot occur during a full moon. Thallus wrote in the middle of the first century, seemingly referring to the events of Christ's crucifixion, although he apparently attempted to explain it by natural causes.

Can the Gospels Be Trusted?

The most obvious place to begin is both the best and worst place to start. The best is obvious: the New Testament has by far the most information about what Jesus actually said and did. Why the worst? Because the Gospels suffer unmitigated criticism as biased, agenda-driven productions that are full of legends, myths, and outright lies. The ill-treatment of the Gospels is almost shocking. Can they be trusted? There are several marks we can go by to see the reliability of the Gospels:

The authors had nothing to gain and did not profit from their work. The biblical authors would have gained nothing from publishing their Gospels. In fact, it would have been quite the opposite. Friction between Christians and their Roman rulers grew increasingly heated as the first century progressed. Peter and Paul are thought to have been martyred in the early 60s, while the synoptic Gospels were published shortly thereafter. John published his Gospel a decade or two later. Their work would have served as a lightning rod for persecution, which gradually increased in intensity over the first couple of centuries AD.

The authors include embarrassing details about Jesus. Jesus is considered sinless, yet He is baptized. Because the apostles claimed that one must be baptized for the forgiveness of sins (Acts 2:38), some might mistakenly believe that Jesus was also baptized for forgiveness of His sin. Why include a scene that could be so easily misunderstood? Jesus dies the shameful death of a criminal that would have been perceived as disqualifying Him as the Messiah by the Jewish populace (cf. Deuteronomy 21:22, 23). Why not depict him dying as a martyr rather than suffering the fate of a criminal? Finally, two women discover the empty tomb. The testimony of women in Roman court was viewed as unreliable. If this is really made up, why not have the apostles discover the empty tomb first?

The authors include embarrassing details about the apostles. The Gospels frequently include details that would have been an embarrassment to the fledgling Christian movement. The apostles are frequently depicted as dull-headed and not really grasping who Christ was until after the resurrection. Thomas is famous for his doubt. It's likely that everyone else doubted as much as he did, but he was the only one who admitted it. The apostles were frequently rebuked by Jesus (Mark 16:14), and Peter more than most (Matthew 16:23). James and John were rebuked by Jesus as well (Luke 9:54, 55), with Matthew reporting that He did so after their mother got involved (Matthew 20:20-28). If the two had any self-respect, one would think they would try to exercise their apostolic authority to keep this little gem out of the official record.

Objecting to Jesus

While the New Testament documents date extremely early and far outstrip any other work in ancient history, there remain four questions about the Gospels, which we will now explore.

The Gospels were written anonymously. Critics frequently claim that the Gospels were originally written anonymously, which is echoed by a few scholars. However, ancient writers usually attached their names to their work. That the Gospels should be identified with their authors stems from two main arguments. First, the early church was virtually unanimous on the authorship of the Gospels. The Synoptic Gospels are virtually uncontested. This would not be the case if the Gospels were written anonymously. One would expect there to be a great deal of debate if no one had any idea who wrote them.

Second, the Gospels were attributed to lesser figures in the early church. Matthew, Mark, and Luke receive very little attention outside the Gospels. If one were to attribute something as important as the biography of Jesus to anyone, we would expect it to be attributed to one of the superstars of the Christian movement, as was the custom in later times with extrabiblical gospels. Authors of the apocryphal and pseudepigraphal books frequently chose popular luminaries such as Peter, Paul, James, or Barnabas as the supposed authors of these uninspired books.

Jesus' disciples were illiterate. While many of Jesus' followers may have been illiterate, it certainly wasn't the case for Matthew and Luke. A customs official and a physician, respectively, these two men would have had the ability to read and write. Mark was from a well-to-do family, which usually meant that he would have had the opportunity for a quality education. The only exception is John. His Gospel is in fairly rough Greek, what one might expect a fisherman to use.

Tradition was not preserved accurately. The transmission of the New Testament is frequently compared to a game of "broken telephone" in which a line of people takes turns whispering a phrase from one person to the next. After reaching the end of the line, the message has been garbled beyond recognition, much to the delight of the participants. This is a terrible analogy. The Gospels were written within the living memory of those who saw the events firsthand, and plenty of eyewitnesses would have had the opportunity to contradict the Gospels if the authors had gotten their facts wrong. We do not hear of this in the early church. The transmission of the Gospels was not a hushed whisper to one individual but a written record presented during the lifetimes of the eyewitnesses.

A second factor in favor of the accurate transmission of the Gospels, especially Jesus' teachings, is the fact that the events took place in an oral culture. This is often its largest target for criticism but is actually one of its greatest strengths. People living in oral cultures routinely possess a far better memory than those living in highly literate societies. A literate culture possesses the ability to write things down and enjoy the luxury of not having to remember anything. This was not the case in the ancient world where memory was prized.

Several factors converge to demonstrate the reliability of the records of Jesus' teaching. First, early writers prized the "living voice." Personal accounts were preferred over written ones, precisely because a presentation communicates much more information than words on a page. One can benefit from tone, inflection, and gesticulation in an oral presentation. Second, it has been estimated that Jesus' words are at least 80 percent poetic in nature, which would lend itself to easy remembrance. Finally, the disciples would have followed Jesus for several years. As an itinerant rabbi frequently speaking to fresh crowds, the disciples likely heard much of the same material a number of times. Like any speaker who teaches the same lessons over and over, Jesus likely taught with much the same inflection, tone, and vocabulary each time, which would further lend itself to easy memorization.

Short Shrift For Jesus?

Many critics ask why more writers do not refer to Jesus. In spite of the wealth of evidence from ancient sources, David Mills asks, "There is not a single reference to a 'Jesus' or to 'Jesus Christ' written by any secular source who lived during the years in which Christ supposedly walked the earth. To me, this fact is very revealing, since these years represent one of the most thoroughly documented periods in antiquity."[xii] In other words, there were plenty of writers in the first century AD, so why didn't more of them mention Jesus if He was so popular?

Not so fast, David. We have to look at things in their proper context. The Gospels consistently portray Christ as being popular with average people, the very ones to whom He came to minister. The only time He attracted national attention was during His crucifixion. In the eyes of Rome He was a political insurrectionist executed as a criminal of the state. Why would the historians, who generally belonged to the elite class of society, bother wasting valuable space on someone considered to be a dead felon? Their readers weren't interested in stories of executed Jewish convicts. The real surprise is that Roman writers mention Him at all.

A second problem with Mills' criticism is that if his standard were to be applied to modern-day writers, no one should be permitted to write any history of events prior to his or her lifetime. If a historian has to actually witness the events firsthand, then this leaves only a tiny window of time about which they can write. If all history is suspect unless the writer has seen things with his own eyes, then we can know almost nothing about the past.

When we examine the life of Christ, we immediately see an unfair double standard at work. One could as much argue that Socrates never existed. Though he is considered a pivotal figure in ancient Greek philosophy, Socrates, like Jesus, was a popular teacher but did not leave a single word of writing behind. What scholars have is the presentation of Socrates in the writings of Plato and Xenophon, along with his depiction in a play of Aristophanes titled *Clouds*. In each of the three, the presentation of the man is noticeably different. Contemporary Greek historians do not mention him, and his trial goes unmentioned in official sources. The two accounts of the trial in Plato and Xenophon frequently contradict each other. If we were to use the same standards used against the Gospels, we would be forced to conclude that Socrates is even less likely to have existed than Jesus.

The difference between Jesus and Socrates comes down to the principle of *coherence*. Scholars examine the data we have on Jesus—in this case, the four Gospels—and try to determine whether the writers present a consistent picture of Jesus. The Gospels give different angles on one man; the Greek sources on Socrates almost seem to be speaking about three different men. Despite this lack of consistency, Socrates is deemed historical, while Jesus is not.

In spite of the evidence, it is often stated in popular sources that Jesus never existed. One has to look pretty hard to find scholars who will argue that Jesus never lived. Even scholars that most Christians would regard as skeptics would argue that He did live. There are too many first and second century references to Jesus. In terms of extrabiblical writings, there are about a dozen that date to within a century of Jesus' death that mention Him.

What Do You Do With Jesus?

The majority of those who deny the historicity of Jesus are either atheist, agnostic, or hold to a form of pseudo-Christianity that has no need for the resurrection. While this sounds obvious, it reveals a potential explanation for why so many reject the historicity of Jesus. As we stated above, there is just as much, if not better, evidence for Jesus than for other historical figures such as Socrates, or other religious figures such as Krishna, Confucius, or the Buddha. Only historical skeptics question the existence of other figures, but many more question the existence of Jesus. Why?

One potential explanation is that Jesus established ethical demands for the individual, and claimed the backing of divine authority in doing so. If Jesus really lived then He really claimed that people are to change their behavior. The teachings of any given philosopher or religious guru may be accepted, modified, or abandoned without penalty. Only Jesus established a code of belief and conduct that is as unalterable as its author. The acceptance or rejection of that code is grounds for either eternal reward or eternal punishment. The implications of how one responds to Jesus are infinitely different from how one responds to any of the world's great sages or wise men.

The absolute nature of Jesus' claims may provide the reason that so many have denied His historicity. Nothing in the last few decades has been as liberating for unbelief as the "death of God," as Nietzsche put it. In reading the accounts of believers who have conceded their faith, it never fails that once their faith is gone the individual expresses the overwhelming feeling of liberation. For these individuals, heaven can be had on earth not by subjection *to* God, but freedom *from* Him.

Jesus Really Lived

It was not until modern times that anyone—scholar or not—denied the historicity of Jesus. Even in the earliest days of Christianity it never seemed to cross anyone's mind that the easiest way to dispel the "Christian problem" would be to deny that Jesus ever lived. Where did such a strong belief come from, if it did not stem from actual events? Historian Will Durant, who was a secularist and avowed agnostic, says, "That a few simple men should in one generation have invented so powerful and appealing a personality, so lofty and ethic and so inspiring a vision of human brotherhood, would be a miracle far more incredible than any recorded in the Gospels."[xiii]

Truth 7

Jesus Was Raised from the Dead

A cartoon depicts a zombie with a halo munching down on a little boy's head. In a word bubble the boy says, "Why is my messiah trying to eat my brain?" The caption beneath the picture reads, "After three days, Jesus was raised from the tomb." In a clear reference to George Romero's horror classic *The Night of the Living Dead*, the cartoonist lampoons the idea of Jesus' resurrection. It isn't far off the mark from the charges of critics today.

The idea that Jesus was raised from the dead immediately separates Him from every other teacher. Among the world's religions, there is no other spiritual leader or guru who is resurrected from the dead. Consequently, some religious teachers try to promote a different kind of Jesus. The Reverend Sun Myung Moon, leader of the Unification Church, teaches that Jesus was the "second Adam" who only fulfilled part of his mission. Moon, as the "third Adam" must complete the work that Jesus left unfinished. Charles Taze Russell, founder of the Jehovah's Witnesses, taught that Christ was none other than the incarnate angel Michael. Muhammad taught that Jesus did not suffer crucifixion but that someone else died in His place (Sura 4:156-158). Most simply assert that Jesus stayed put in the tomb after His burial.

One of the most important events in Christ's life on earth was His resurrection from the tomb. For critics, this ranks among the most laughable features of the Christian faith. For Christians, it is one of the most important. Which one is right?

Many object to the idea that Jesus was raised from the dead saying that this goes against known fact. Generally, that is true. You won't ever see a news broadcast covering a true resurrection. Human beings don't just get up out of their coffins. But was there a unique event two thousand years ago where God intervened and resurrected someone? If we close off the doors of our minds and barricade them with philosophical naturalism, then the answer will be a resounding "no." But if we allow the evidence to speak for itself without filtering it, what does it say?

Testimony from the Disciples

When reading the gospel accounts of Jesus' death, it is immediately apparent that the small band of disciples is thrown into complete disarray. They are downtrodden and disillusioned after having seen their teacher executed as a criminal. In their minds, it might be similar to watching the spectacular public downfalls of televangelists like Jim Bakker, Jimmy Swaggart, and Ted Haggard. Christians are accustomed to looking at the cross with 20/20 hindsight colored with the nobility and purpose of Christ's death. To those who were there to see it firsthand, it was like watching a prison warden strap a death row inmate into an electric chair and throw the switch.

There are a number of different perspectives on Jesus in the modern world, but in the first century Jesus would not have been seen in a positive light. In fact, His manner of death would have led most Jews to believe that Jesus was not only a failed Messiah but a false one. We understand the disillusionment of the disciples after Jesus' death, because they thought He was really dead. The two

Jesus Was Raised from the Dead

disciples on the road to Damascus demonstrate the downtrodden attitude of the disciples perfectly (Luke 24:17-21), as does the skepticism of Thomas (John 20:25).

In only a short time, however, the disciples are traveling the coastline of the Mediterranean world preaching the death and resurrection of Christ at great personal expense. Paul is stoned, beaten, and shipwrecked, all listed in a medical file of injuries worse than that of any professional athlete (2 Corinthians 11:23-28). The book of Acts records high levels of hostility against the apostles and early believers (cf. Acts 7:54-60; 8:1-3; 12:1-3), of whom all but one was likely executed. Only John died a natural death, alone and in exile. Tradition says that James, the brother of Jesus, was murdered in cold blood. Early evangelists did not have a long life expectancy. Neither did many ordinary Christians.

One might object to the reaction of the disciples, arguing that other religions have their devotees as well. Religious beliefs can and do change people's lives whether or not they are Christian. Extremist Muslims are willing to engage in Jihad and blow themselves up in the pursuit of paradise. Disciples, such as those of Gandhi, are willing to defy the natural fight-or-flight response to persecution and death in their steadfast commitment to nonviolence. The Heaven's Gate cult went so far as to commit mass suicide in order to catch an outbound flight on a UFO. Can a change really signal a proof that the belief is true? Not exactly.

The most that a person's commitment is able to prove is that they believe that their beliefs are true. After all, no one suffers for beliefs they understand to be false. The difference is trying to determine the difference between the attitudes of the early Christians and those of other believers. Many religions have the power to transform the lives of believers. But early Christians saw something that transformed them in a thoroughly unexpected way. Many saw Jesus as a failed Messiah. He had encouraged them His with wonderful teachings, only to wind up getting killed by the Romans. Christians were convinced by something after they had been given irrefutable proof that their beliefs were misplaced. Only the resurrection would have the power to do that.

The early Christians had beliefs just like any other religious person. The difference is that they received confirmation of those beliefs when they thought that all hope was lost. Even James and Paul—both of whom were skeptical of Jesus, to say the least—wound up being convinced. It is important to note here that scholars do not deny the existence or commitment of either from a combination of the Bible, tradition, and historical sources.

Skeptics are at a loss to explain the post-resurrection appearance of Jesus. Eyewitness reports of the resurrection from the sources we have are very early and would not have had time to grow out of legendary accounts passed from one person to the next over time. They appear within several years after Christ's death. Second, explanations for the empty tomb that have appeared in the last two centuries are not considered credible even by liberal scholars. Examples would be the swoon theory (Jesus passed out on the cross and was entombed while still alive and escaped later) and the stolen body theory (which does not account for eyewitness reports of Christ's resurrection). Christians are left with one explanation: Jesus actually was raised from the dead.

There are several odd pieces of historical evidence that support the resurrection. First, Joseph of Arimathea buries Jesus in his personal tomb. This would be seen as a strange thing because Joseph belonged to the Sanhedrin, the very court that had condemned Jesus to die. Second, the empty tomb is discovered by two women, which would have been equally odd to early believers. The testimony of women was considered unreliable, yet the two women serve as the primary witnesses to the empty tomb. No one would have made this up. It would make much better sense for Peter, James, and John to have discovered the empty tomb because the women's story easily could have been seen as a fantastic product of the women's imagination (cf. Matt. 28:1-10; Luke 24:1-11). While Esther and Ruth were great examples of heroic Jewish women,

Mary Magdalene and her companion (the "other Mary") were anything but national heroes. Third, belief in the resurrection of Jesus is both immediate and goes against their own expectations. The disciples watched Jesus die after failing to meet popular expectations that Jews had of the Messiah. The very sentence of crucifixion was enough for most to conclude that Jesus was a fraud. Yet in short order the disciples undergo a remarkable transformation and are willing to die for Christ even though Jewish expectations were that resurrection would only happen at the end of time. Finally, the early Jewish opposition to the empty tomb demonstrates that there is some knowledge of the vacated tomb. Earliest Christianity could have been squashed easily if all the Jewish authorities had to do was produce Christ's body. The church would have been as lifeless as the corpse of its founder.

Firsthand Accounts of the Empty Tomb

The most compelling evidence for the resurrection of Christ is borne out in the lives of His apostles and biographers. The Gospels were written within one or two generations of Christ's death, meaning that there were living witnesses who could dispute the official version of the crucifixion and resurrection. If anyone questioned the accounts of the resurrection, there were plenty of people available who could have set the record straight.

The Gospels weren't just biographies—they were lightning rods for discrimination and even persecution. Some try to mitigate this evidence with the frequently repeated charge that the Gospels were written anonymously, but the ancient church knew exactly who wrote the Gospels, and the Romans could have found out just as easily. Attaching the author's name to the outside page or to a tag on the document was standard practice. If the church wanted to make the Gospels acceptable, they would have attributed them to the superstars of the church, not to lesser luminaries like Luke and Mark. Virtually no disagreement exists about who wrote each Gospel. If they had been produced truly anonymously, we would expect centuries-long battles over authorship. Instead, we find barely a trace of disagreement.

Remember that by the time the Gospels were being written by Mark, Luke, and Matthew, a number of witnesses who had heard the first reports of the empty tomb and perhaps even seen the risen Christ were still alive. Stories of the resurrection and the resurrected Christ would have already been in circulation for a generation before the earliest Gospel was written. If the resurrection of Christ were simply an invention foisted upon the church, we would expect others to deny it. Actually, there is something similar to this in the first century.

Apollonius of Tyana is a relatively famous first-century figure whose followers butted heads with the early Christians. His followers credited him with performing miracles such as healing the sick, including supposedly raising a dead girl back to life. Many critics cite Apollonius as one example of the wonder-working sage who is later deified after his death as a parallel for Christ. In doing so, the uniqueness of Christ is diminished. There is one unavoidable problem with this approach, however. Many of Apollonius' miracles were contested by his own followers. His greatest miracle, the supposed resurrection of a child, was perhaps the most disputed of all. Because Apollonius is considered a parallel to Christ, one would expect his followers to demonstrate the same commitment to him that the early Christians devoted to Christ. The contrast between the responses of Jesus' and Appolonius' followers indicates something special about the ministry of Christ.

The resurrection of Jesus is also seen in the message of the apostles. In fact, it is a central feature of the first recorded gospel sermon of Peter in Acts 2. The apostle spends considerable time in his sermon focused on the death of Jesus and its liberating effects from the power of sin. Paul claims that a number of witnesses saw the risen Christ (1 Corinthians 15:3-8). While Paul does not explicitly mention the empty tomb, his statement that Jesus was raised from the dead certainly implies the empty tomb (cf. Romans 1:3-4;

10:9). Just as important, Paul is writing that more than five hundred witnesses saw Jesus at one time (1 Corinthians 15:6); indicating that Jesus appeared to a large number of people and was not just a tall tale told by a select few. The apostle invites the entire Corinthian church to investigate the matter and draw their own conclusions.

The apostles preached the resurrection of Jesus which converted thousands. It would make no sense that people would believe Jesus had risen from death if His corpse had been dragged through the streets. Likewise, if Jesus' body was in the possession of the authorities, there would be little effort needed to produce the body and immediately invalidate the message of the apostles. The Christian movement could have easily been squashed before it ever took root. The fact that it wasn't implies that the authorities did not have any proof to refute the resurrection.

There is a later explanation of the empty tomb. *Toledoth Jesu* is a late document giving an alternate version of what happened to Jesus' body. According to this anti-Christian piece, a gardener stole Jesus' body from the tomb, causing the disciples to think He had risen from the grave. This man later gave it to Jewish leaders who dragged the body through the streets of Jerusalem. Because the work was authored in the fifth century and the weight of evidence refutes the claim, it is an untrustworthy source; although it may preserve some memory of Christ in the Gospels' presentation of His death.

What the Resurrection Means for Christians

Some have objected to the burial of Jesus in the tomb, arguing that Jesus' body would have been left exposed on the cross and eaten by vultures or thrown into a trench to be eaten by wild dogs. There are several objections to this. The Jewish philosopher Philo, a contemporary of Paul, tells a story of a special case where the body of a crucifixion victim was given to his family for burial just prior to a festival.[i] In another case, archaeologists discovered the ossuary (bone box) of a crucifixion victim named Yehohanan. That he was crucified is evident because the nail used to fix his feet to the cross was found still embedded in one of his heel bones.

The primary objection to the resurrection of Jesus comes not from evidence but from philosophy. Critics almost always hold a naturalistic philosophical viewpoint that excludes all supernatural events. There is usually no good explanation given for such a stance, and none is offered. In the nineteenth century, critics supplied naturalistic explanations of biblical miracles. When Jesus walked on the water (Matthew 14:25; Mark 6:48; John 6:19), it was really because He found a hidden sandbar just underneath the waves to walk upon. Jesus survived crucifixion and "resurrected" because Luke slipped Him a drug that only simulated His death. It is good procedure to rely on naturalistic explanations if they are the best fit with the evidence; but in the case of the resurrection, natural explanations fail to be convincing. Something more must have been at work.

This naturalistic mindset governs the view of history held by virtually all critics. The Bible cannot be true, they argue, because miracles don't happen. So what is the evidence that miracles don't happen? None. Everybody knows it already, so there's no need to provide proof. It is a case of unsubstantiated claims arising out of an unquestioned, anti-supernatural worldview. What is even more disappointing is that this preconceived bias is every bit as dogmatic as any religious worldview. New Testament scholar Michael Bird writes,

> In Bertolt Brecht's play *Life of Galileo*, Galileo is trying to prove to some friends that the earth revolves around the sun and not vice versa, and he tells his friends that all they have to do is look through the telescope and they'll be able to see all the evidence they need. Yet before looking through the telescope his friends decide to have a scientific disputation first to determine whether or not the hypothesis of a non-Ptolemaic universe is in fact possible; they decide that it isn't possible and therefore refuse to look

through the telescope at all ... those who think that religion has a monopoly on dogmatism better think again....[ii]

Notice that last sentence. Religion is not the sole proprietor of dogmatism. The critic is just as dogmatic, and it doesn't stop others from criticizing the reality of the resurrection, regardless of whether it is in modern or ancient times. The Greek satirist Lucian of Samosata made fun of Christians because they believed in eternal life. He said,

> The Christians, you know, worship a man to this day—the distinguished personage who introduced their novel rites, and was crucified on that account.... You see, these misguided creatures start with the general conviction that they are immortal for all time, which explains the contempt of death and voluntary self-devotion which are so common among them ....[iii]

It was the righteous contempt for death born from Christ's resurrection that transformed the trembling disciples into crusading apostles. These men had seen their Savior die, and according to the Jewish thinking of the day Jesus was not only a failed messiah but a false one. Everything about Jesus' death as an executed felon screamed at the disciples, "Go put your faith somewhere else!" Yet something happened to ignite a fire within these men that could only be quenched by preaching Christ and Him not only crucified (1 Corinthians 1:13) but resurrected.

Christians remember the death of Christ every week in communion. An idea often overlooked is that Christ was not only raised from the dead but currently reigns at the right hand of God. It gives the hope that the Christian, too, will rise from the grave, no longer subject to the power of death. In Christ humanity finds the cure for death, the universal terminal disease.

Men On Fire

So was Jesus really raised from the dead? The question we have to ask is this: What explanation best accounts for the evidence? Clearly something had to happen after Jesus' death to generate the reports of His resurrection. A belief this monumental doesn't appear out of thin air.

Jesus is mentioned in both biblical and extrabiblical sources. No reputable scholar denies that Jesus actually walked the earth or was crucified under Pontius Pilate. The only people who deny this are often agenda-driven non-specialists, many of whom draw upon non-scholarly sources. Remember that those who spend lifetimes studying the firsthand material, even when they are unbelievers, still affirm the basic story presented in the Gospels.

The Bible describes the dramatic turnaround of the disciples. The Gospels portray the disciples as weak, fearful, and timid after Christ's death. Very soon, they transform into emboldened evangelists scouring the eastern Mediterranean. There must have been a nearly life-altering event to enact such a transformation, especially because they are willing to give their lives for what they believed. If Jesus was not raised from the dead, the apostles' willingness to die for a fabricated hoax would be explainable only by sheer insanity. As the old saying goes, liars make poor martyrs.

Early Christians were very influential. Though the followers of Christ watched their Savior die, the church explodes across the Mediterranean. Twenty years later the Christians are in Rome, and the name of Christ is known by the Roman emperor Claudius. Eighty years later, the Roman governor Pliny knows them well enough to be familiar with their beliefs and activities and also mentions that they are so influential that they have made a dramatic impact on the local pagan cults. These and other writers were members of the Roman elite, yet the Christian movement was popular enough to grab their attention. This doesn't sound like a movement based on a dead criminal.

Extrabiblical sources are familiar with the resurrection of Christ. Even writers who are hostile to Christianity know the stories of Christ's resurrection. Though they may try to downplay or disparage the resurrection story, their familiarity with it is an important witness.

The success of the early church was not guaranteed. It wasn't even very likely. A host of problems faced the budding church in the first century. Still, these people tenaciously hung onto the belief that their Lord had defeated the power of death itself and that one day they would rise above it as well. What could have possibly led these people to meet in secret at their own peril, suffer discrimination and persecution, and forsake friends and family for their beliefs? Perhaps we can trace it back to an unexpected surprise one morning two thousand years ago when a few women discovered the power of God in an empty tomb.

Truth 8

Evil, Pain, and Suffering Do Not Disprove God's Existence

I remember watching television one night when the anchor of the nightly news came on. He said that this particular night was special, and announced, "There's no bad news to report!" My eyes widened, and I shot straight up in my seat. This was going to be one of those nights that people look back twenty years from now and ask, "Do you remember what you were doing when …?" Most people remember what they were doing when JFK was shot, Elvis died, the Challenger space shuttle exploded, or terrorists flew planes into the World Trade Center on September 11, 2001. I was certain I would never forget this one night in the history of news broadcasting that no bad news would travel across the airwaves.

I anxiously awaited the anchorman's comments. But the next sentence that came out of his mouth floored me. He said that he wished it were so; he wished there was a day with no bad news. But then he reminded us all that whenever we needed news updates to be sure and tune in to his station. It was just a promotional gimmick! I sank back into my seat. I had just been on an emotional rollercoaster that made the biggest monstrosity at Six Flags look like a merry-go-round. After having a few moments to think about it, I felt ripped off. Cheated. But in the end, after I thought about it, I decided that bad things were not just something found in the world every day but are an inescapable part of life on planet Earth.

No matter how hard we try, it seems we can never get away from bad news. People hungry for news are fed a steady diet of villainy. We see pictures in third-world countries of emaciated people whose starved bodies litter the streets. The walking dead vainly shoo away the host of pests that alight upon their blighted bodies. Every channel is racing to give us breaking news of the latest terrorist attack, the most recent mugging, or last night's murder.

Why, God?

Terminal disease, violent crime, and a seemingly infinite number of other wicked deeds create a cacophony of evil played in the symphony house of a world as black as midnight. So where is God, you ask? If God is truly good and wants to help His people, why won't He help us? Francis Schaeffer titled one of his books *He is There, and He is Not Silent*. Really? The mass of evil in the world gives every appearance that God is either deaf or indifferent.

While everyone experiences pain in their lifetime on Earth, this issue has perhaps the greatest impact because of the raw nature of human emotions. The existential suffering experienced by millions on a daily basis leaves them questioning, "Why?" Through prayer they send their question up to the starry host receiving only silence for an answer.

One of the greatest arguments against the existence of God is the reality of evil, pain, and suffering. Many atheists cite a negative personal experience as the reason for leaving the faith or for bolstering their rationale for never accepting God in the first place. This is reflected in part by the OmniPoll, conducted by the Barna

Evil, Pain, and Suffering Do Not Disprove God's Existence

Research Group in January 1999, which asked, "If you could ask God only one question and you knew he would give you an answer, what would you ask?" The top response, given by 17 percent of respondents, was "Why is there so much pain and suffering?"[i]

In the book *The Case for Faith*, Lee Strobel interviews Charles Templeton about the moment he lost his faith. When asked about the one thing that caused him to lose his faith, Templeton replied, "It was a photograph in *Life* magazine." When asked to explain,

> He narrowed his eyes a bit and looked off to the side, as if he were viewing the photo afresh and reliving the moment. "It was a picture of a black woman in Northern Africa," he explained. "They were experiencing a devastating drought. And she was holding her dead baby in her arms and looking up to heaven with the most forlorn expression. I looked at it and I thought, 'Is it possible to believe that there is a loving or caring Creator when all this woman needed was *rain*'...Who else but a fiend could destroy a baby and virtually kill its mother with agony—when all that was needed was *rain*?"[ii]

At first glance, it appears that an all-powerful good God cannot co-exist with evil. Here we see the doomsday conundrum posed by the critic. "Why doesn't God help? You Christians say he is all-powerful and perfectly good. He does not help. That is obvious. The question is why. Either he is all-powerful but not good enough to eradicate evil, or he is really that good but isn't powerful enough to do so. So which is it?"

In the book of Genesis, the Bible explains clearly that the intent of God is goodness. It is humanity that breaches the agreement with God in Genesis 3 by eating the forbidden fruit. Humanity opens wide the door for suffering. In the beginning, evil is merely a potentiality. It is humanity who *actualizes* it.

So why does God even permit the possibility of evil? He made His creatures with the freedom to make their own choices. If God wanted a race of robots incapable of sinning or unable to experience suffering, He could have done that. We would all be mindless automatons who could never violate our programming. We would always do what we were told, never deviating from our instructions. We would have to be told what to do, when, where, and with whom. In short, we would never have freedom.

Instead, God created the human race with the ability to make contrary choices. It never ceases to amaze me how strong our desire to choose for ourselves really is. When my daughter was four years old, she wanted to do everything on her own. We heard the tireless refrain, "I want to do it all by myself!" Young or old, everyone wants freedom. But that freedom comes with responsibility, because freedom of choice permits love but also permits the possibility of evil. If love can be freely given, then it can also be freely abused.

As C.S. Lewis once wrote, "Free will, though it makes evil possible, is also the only thing that makes possible any love or goodness or joy worth having. A world of automata—of creatures that worked like machines—would hardly be worth creating."[iii] A world of mindless drones would be one in which human beings would have no more value than simple machines. Freedom is the hallmark of value. Though it doesn't offer a complete explanation for the problem of evil, it does offer an explanation for evil resulting from human choices.

He Never Said It Would Be Easy

The emotional component of the problem of evil, pain, and suffering is exactly what makes it so dangerous. When former believers are polled about what made them turn their backs on God, one inevitable response is that some hardship had been suffered in the past that made them question God's existence. This is very much the case with Bart Ehrman, a former minister who wrote a book entitled *God's Problem: How the Bible Fails to Answer Our Most*

Evil, Pain, and Suffering Do Not Disprove God's Existence

Important Question—Why We Suffer in which he explores the problem of pain and suffering. Raised in a fundamentalist Christian home, Ehrman later renounced his faith when writing his doctoral dissertation at Princeton Theological Seminary.[iv] He taught part-time for Rutgers University, when one semester he was asked to teach a course called, "The Problem of Suffering in the Biblical Traditions." He impressed upon his students the reality of suffering in the world, and in doing so seemed to have started down the path toward unbelief. Today, unable to reconcile the reality of suffering with a good God, he simply resigns himself to agnosticism.

When humanity falls in Genesis 3, curses come down from on high. It is only then that true suffering enters the world. Woman experiences pain in childbirth and frustration in attempting to rule over her husband, while man eats of the ground only by the sweat of his brow. Life is irrevocably altered not only for Adam and Eve, but for all who will follow them.

But what about senseless tragedy? That's the question. A mother sobs as she clutches her stillborn child. Relatives tearfully identify the body of a loved one in a morgue. News comes that a son or daughter has just been killed in a car accident. A family visits the remains of a house full of memories devoured by fire, earthquake, flood, or tornado. And though these mourners have never met, their hearts cry out in a single chorus of agony. What do we say?

Doesn't a life full of suffering demonstrate that God cannot exist? Actually, we could turn that around and ask the opposite question. "If there is no God, why is there so much good?" If we look at the animal kingdom (from which we supposedly evolved) to provide noble ethics, we wouldn't find much.

Human beings can be cruel too. It isn't too hard to think of some of the most godless societies on earth, mainly because they are also the ones who are most infamous for causing widespread human suffering. We can think of the French Revolution under Robespierre, the first society to be constructed as atheist from the foundation upward. The removal of God, defacement of churches and religious artwork, and deification of Reason characterized this period in French history. So did bloodshed thanks to the newly invented guillotine.

The twentieth century saw more than its share of death thanks to godless nations like Nazi Germany, who executed Jews, homosexuals, and religious folk by the millions. Soviet Russia was no different. Tens of millions died under Stalin and millions more slaved away in gulags (forced labor camps) for crimes as simple as telling anti-government jokes or having too many unexcused absences from work. In North Korea millions starved while its dictator dined in sumptuous luxury. We could look to Zimbabwe and Rwanda and dozens of other countries like them for an indescribable portrait of horror. Wherever God has been exiled from the public square, the devil's hands have been busy.

Some of the worst suffering imaginable is emotional. Unfortunately, human beings also like to shift blame, making others responsible for their suffering. In a sense, it is natural. Human beings try to understand things that happen in life, to make sense of what happens. We instinctively look for causes and seek ways to put that information in perspective. So when we suffer, we look to find the root of why. We have an imaginary construct of God in our minds, that if God exists and loves us, then He should be willing to exercise a tiny bit of His unfathomably immense power to make our lives better. After all, if we had that power, wouldn't we do the same? Well, maybe not.

Sometimes popular thinking has a surprisingly acute level of theological insight. In the movie *Bruce Almighty*, God (played by Morgan Freeman) gives a local news reporter divine power. When he starts hearing the prayers of every individual within the radius of a few city blocks, he decides to set up the prayers in the form of e-mails. When he discovers that he has untold millions of "prayer-mails" to answer, he simply hits "Reply to All" and answers, "Yes!" Pure chaos ensues. The streets are overcome with total anarchy. In one example, millions of prayers are answered for people playing the lottery, which means that no one gets more than a few dollars. Why doesn't God answer every prayer today? Because there are greater things God is trying to accomplish in the world. Everyone prays for great things, and everyone prays for selfish things. If God answered every prayer uttered by human lips, human society would descend into primeval chaos.

Good and Evil

In the end, the problem behind the argument against God's existence on the basis of the existence of evil is that the critic must show why the existence of evil and God are mutually exclusive. There must be some contradiction involved in the co-existence of God and evil in order for this argument to prove successful. The problem with this argument, like many different arguments used against the Christian faith, is that the critics confidently announce what is posed as a difficult problem. It is the believer who assumes that the charge must be answered and takes it upon himself to connect the dots and go on the defensive. A very simple way to counter arguments of this type would be to ask the simple question, "Why?"

Though evil is a powerful force, there is something else even more powerful: hope. The Bible teaches that while evil and suffering seem to be prevalent in the world today, there is a day coming in which evil will be eradicated forever.

Some might object, saying, "Justice delayed is justice denied! What happens in the here and now, where billions suffer evils and cruelties every day? If I were God, I'd end it all now!" Expediency is a goal of American jurisprudence, but God works on a different timetable.

Human-centered arguments beginning with the words, "If I were God ..." are almost always emotionally driven and fundamentally arrogant. So what if we were God? How would we make things any different? We have to take great care in how we answer that question, because we cannot give a pat answer like, "I'd create a world without evil." Without understanding why evil is in *this* world, why would we be so arrogant to think we could or would create a world without it if we were divine?

When examining the problem of evil, pain, and suffering, critics generally miss the fact that God did not exempt Himself from pain. Scripture is replete with examples of God experiencing His own discomfort. In most cases, it is the refusal of His people to show fundamental decency and respect. The most important incident, however, is the cross. It is difficult to imagine God standing dispassionately in heaven unmoved by the shameful treatment of His Son in life and the torture of His excruciating death. Some say that the pain of losing a child is the greatest that a person can experience. God knows all about it and on a level that is completely inconceivable by human beings. The fact that God did not spare Himself suffering means that there must be a greater purpose to its existence.

We realize that in all aspects of life some of the greatest achievements in human history have been in the worst situations. Why is it that we respect the powerful born with silver spoons in their mouths, but reserve our greatest admiration for those who achieved no less by pulling themselves up by their own bootstraps? Moral character, endurance, and courage are found by overcoming negative circumstances and by maturing through challenges and hardships. James the brother of Jesus records that there is purpose to hardships and trials in the Christian faith as well. He says that testing one's faith develops perseverance (James 1:2-5). He also says that those who weather trials are blessed (v. 12).

Death ultimately is meaningless, yet we attribute great meaning to self-sacrifice. On the morning of April 16, 2007, twenty-three-year-old Virginia Tech student Cho Seung-Hui armed himself with two firearms and several hundred rounds of ammunition. He made his way through two buildings on campus, indiscriminately shooting professors and his fellow students. In room 204 in Norris Hall, engineering professor and Holocaust survivor Liviu Librescu barricaded the door to allow his students to escape. The students raced for the windows while Librescu shouted at them to hurry. Librescu died after being hit from gunfire as Cho fired through the door. After the incident, the professor was regarded as a hero.

The fact that we conceive of the difference between evil and good points in the direction of God's existence. If we are nothing more than sophisticated versions of lions and gazelles, we wouldn't have any problem with thieves, rapists, and murderers. The fact that we recognize evil means that we understand there is a standard.

In *Dialogues Concerning Natural Religion*, David Hume wrote,

> Were a stranger to drop, in a sudden, into this world, I would show him as a specimen of its ills, an hospital full of diseases, a prison crowded with malefactors and debtors, a field of battle strowed with carcasses, a fleet floundering in the ocean, a nation languishing under tyranny, famine, or pestilence. To turn the gay side of life to him, and give him a notion of its pleasures; whither should I conduct him? to a ball, to an opera, to court? He might justly think that I was only showing him a diversity of distress and sorrow.[v]

We could very quickly respond with a number of points. People suffer from disease, but where does the benevolence to care for the suffering come from? Prisons are filled to the brim with those who violate the rights of others, but where does a sense of justice originate? The very fact that Hume decries tyranny, famine, and pestilence attests the fact that these realities are unfair and he can imagine a better place without them.

In the end, the problem of evil is one that has not been given a completely satisfying solution. Is that it, then? The atheist wins? Not so fast. The atheist actually has a problem twice as big as the Christian. Believers may have to explain where evil originates, but the atheist has to explain not only how he or she recognizes evil in the absence of a universal standard of good, but also where that standard originates. If it is nothing more than an opinion, then the truthfulness of that opinion goes no farther than the one holding it. If it is a universal standard, the standard itself requires an explanation.

The fact that every human being innately understands the difference between good and evil points to our creation in the image God. If God is the ultimate standard of goodness and human beings are made in His image (Genesis 1:26), then the ability to discern right and wrong would be a natural one. This recognition is unknown in the animal kingdom. The very fact that the human heart yearns for reprieve amid suffering and justice in the aftermath of unfairness is a secretive testimony to a universal presence of goodness that will one day make Himself known to all.

Truth 9

The Bible Is Inspired

It's undeniable that the Bible is one of the greatest works of literature ever produced. It easily ranks among the great productions from the ancient world regardless of culture, whether Mesopotamian or Egyptian, Greek or Roman. The book of Job is often studied in high school literature classes, and for good reason. Its high literary quality is obvious. But while the Bible is great literature, is it actually the Word of God?

One of the most central aspects of the Christian faith is that God has revealed Himself to man through the Bible. Paul wrote, "All Scripture is breathed out by God" (2 Timothy 3:16). Jesus and the apostles frequently appealed to the Old Testament with the phrase, "it is written." The Old Testament is replete with examples of God directing the writing activity of His writers. God's involvement is also made clear in the prophetic books, which frequently contain the phrase, "Thus says the LORD." It is clear that the biblical writers considered the Bible to be inspired.

Two difficulties face Christians today. First, many who claim to be Christians actually deny the inspiration of large portions of

Scripture. This often comes from those who approach the Bible the same way other scholars study ancient mythology. Second, there are competing voices in the world around us. Other supposed prophets like Joseph Smith, Edgar Cayce, and Jeane Dixon all claimed to speak for God. Our task is to answer the question: Is the Bible any different?

Just Breathe

What is inspiration? It depends on who you ask. Every musician, artist, and poet is looking for some kind of inspiration. Some people refer to it as "finding their muse," a reference to the Nine Muses in Greek mythology who inspired their patrons with abilities in the fine arts. Inspiration is a surge of creativity, focus, or emotion that gives an artist the ability to reach for the stars and to produce something that is uniquely deep and rich for the observer. But what does this mean for the inspiration of Scripture?

Inspiration in biblical terms is fairly different than its meaning elsewhere. Some theologians do not like to use the term in its popular usage at all. In its biblical usage, the connotation of the term is somewhat different than its popular usage. The term *theopneustos* means "God-breathed," as if God breathed truth into the very pages of the Bible itself.

Inspiration as Christians understand it means that God used the Holy Spirit to superintend the writing of Scripture. The Bible is clear that God is directly responsible for the writing of Scripture (2 Peter 1:20, 21), although this does not mean that the writers simply took divine dictation. God prepared His authors to write what they did, but there was also a human element to the writing that took place. The inspiration of the Holy Spirit allowed the biblical authors to use their own vocabularies and experiences as they composed their works.

There are several thousands of instances where the Old Testament claims divine authority by announcing that God is speaking. This may refer to examples where God speaks directly to individuals or where individuals report what they are about to say comes directly from God. In the New Testament, Jesus tells His disciples that they will be given words to speak (Matthew 10:19). Paul indicates in his epistles that he is writing what he has received from God (1 Corinthians 11:23; 1 Thessalonians 4:15).

What is Jesus' view of Scripture? Assuming from our previous discussions that God exists, the Bible is reliable, and Jesus really lived and made accurate claims, we must recognize that Jesus Himself taught that Scripture is inspired. Jesus validates the Old Testament by quoting from the three sections of the Hebrew Bible. The Old Testament as we know it existed in the time of Christ, although the books were arranged quite differently. Organized into the Law, Prophets, and Writings, all of the books that appear in the Hebrew Bible are found in the Old Testament as it exists in Christian Bibles. Jesus not only quotes from each section (Luke 24:44) but also affirms its authority as a whole. This is par for the course with the other figures of the New Testament, including its authors, who claim inspiration for the New Testament as well. Peter notes that Paul's writings are to be considered as authoritative as "Scriptures" (2 Peter 3:15, 16), which means that both the Old Testament and Paul's writings are equally authoritative and equally inspired. Elsewhere, Paul implies that Luke's writing is also Scripture (1 Timothy 5:18).

The Unity of the Bible

One of the greatest demonstrations of the inspiration of the Bible is its remarkable unity. Let's take ten different people and ask them all to write about a given subject. Among the ten writers there may well be ten different opinions, especially if it is a controversial topic. It is a basic facet of human nature that people see things in different ways according to time, place, culture, upbringing, life experiences, and other factors that shape each person's worldview. These very features are reflected in the text of the Bible. For instance, writers like Isaiah and Ezekiel use language that one might expect from priests, because both prophets were also priestly figures. Luke's Gospel and Acts both reflect a writer who was well learned, which fits with the understanding that Luke was a physician. The same goes for Paul, whose epistles are theologically astute. Peter and John were fishermen with little if any formal education. Their Greek is not as elevated as that of Luke.

When we look at the various books of the Bible in the original languages, we see the individual distinctions of the writers come to the surface. Each one has different emphases and uses different vocabulary to communicate different messages. What we do *not* find, however, is different theological or doctrinal positions. This can be appreciated more fully by looking at contemporary examples from the world of the Bible.

In the ancient world, it was not uncommon for religious figures to have vast theological disagreements. There are no less than three competing creation stories from ancient Egypt. The gods Amun, Horus, and Ptah were all asserted to be the most important gods of the Egyptian pantheon by their respective followers. Much the same situation existed in Mesopotamia, where older myths might be rewritten with different gods as the most important for a later audience. In the Babylonian creation myths Marduk is the most important god, but when Assyria dominated the scene the same story was edited so that the Assyrian god Ashur replaced Marduk. One might expect to find different nuances to stories that were inserted by scribes over time. Then again, one might also find gods changing over time or gods from one country being equated with similar gods from another.

Religion in the ancient Near East was rather fluid. Cultures sometimes had several conflicting stories of creation. Local gods might be absorbed by more popular national-level gods and disappear altogether. Deities might reach international status, with the same god going by different names in various countries. The Bible is radically different. We can expect the portrait of God in Scripture to remain much the same whether we are reading Old Testament poetry or a New Testament epistle. Unlike manufactured religions, the theology of the Bible remains consistent over time.

What is even more remarkable is that the portrait painted by the authors of Scripture is consistent in spite of their different backgrounds. The authors of the Bible come from different countries on three different continents (Egypt, Canaan, Persia, Babylonia, Greece), speaking three different languages (Hebrew, Aramaic, Greek), over a span of 1,400 years. Imagine, for instance, taking writers from twenty-first-century America, eighteenth-century England, fifteenth-century Italy, and throw in a couple from medieval Germany and the Egyptian and Persian Empires. Would they have different views on any given topic? Absolutely. That's what makes the Bible's unity so remarkable. It bears a unity unachievable by purely human means.

Is the Bible's unity really all that important? One of the ways to underscore its importance is to examine the history of heresy. It almost appears to be a fundamental aspect of human nature that people disagree, and the reasons for those disagreements are often purely subjective based on the wants and needs of the individual. Let's examine a few cases where the community of faith departed radically from the Bible it claimed.

In looking at the period of the Old Testament, it is easy to see that people often disagree among themselves. Jewish mystics had radically different ideas than those found in the pages of Scripture. The Apocrypha, for instance, contains several ideas that are at odds with biblical teaching. For one, the book of 2 Maccabees glamorizes a Jewish freedom fighter named Razis who commits suicide while evading Roman soldiers. The other apocryphal books make a number of errors with regard to geography, theology, history, and chronology. In the Intertestamental Period, Jewish believers recognized and admitted that God had not spoken since the days of the Hebrew prophets.

The history of the early church is much the same. Other heretical viewpoints, such as Gnosticism, butted heads with Christianity and were ultimately defeated. Gnosticism taught that it was not the work of Christ on the cross but special knowledge that enabled a person to attain salvation. This salvation took the form of freedom from the physical body (which they considered evil) rather than the biblical concept of freedom from the power of sin and death ending in the final and eternal resurrection of the body. Gnostic believers combined Christianity with Greek philosophy, which was rejected by the church.

While the Bible is Jewish from cover to cover, we must point out that more than a thousand years separates its earliest authors (who grew up in the shadows of Egypt and Mesopotamia) from its latest (who were influenced somewhat by Greece). Still, the Bible contains a theology that is harmonious in a way that defies natural explanation.

How Do You Explain...

There are some things about the Bible that defy explanation. One of these areas is in the field of medicine. In the ancient Near East, Egypt was famous for its advancement in the medical arts. Egyptians were considered the leaders in the field. Physicians would go to Egypt to study, and occasionally foreign rulers would bring in an outside specialist from Egypt if their own physicians were stumped.

The ancient Egyptians made genuine attempts at medical diagnosis. They were also quite advanced in the treatments of both illnesses and injuries. The Edwin Smith Surgical Papyrus, for example, lists a number of trauma injuries that a person might sustain, and lists the treatment. If it was a relatively minor injury, the papyrus instructed, "This is an injury which I will treat." If it were serious but treatable, the physician would say, "This is an injury with which I will contend." In severe cases, such as when the skull is fractured and brain matter might be exposed, the physician would be instructed to announce, "This is an injury which I will not treat." The physicians recognized that the more severe the injury, the greater likelihood the patient might die. In the most severe cases, they recognized that no treatment would benefit the patient.

Despite their advances in the medical arts, the Egyptians were susceptible to folk cures and the use of magic. Medicine in ancient

Egypt was advanced for the day but would be seen as quite backward in the twenty-first century. Many of the remedies offered by physicians were actually deadlier than the ailment they aimed to cure. If a person got a splinter, the cure called for different types of dung and worm's blood to be mixed together and applied to the affected area. Because dung contains a vast number of microscopic tetanus spores, this cure was something of a bacteriological time bomb. There was the distinct possibility that the cure could develop into an infection and kill the patient.

Some remedies in the ancient world leave us wondering how the ancients concocted their cures. For instance, in Egypt the remedy for pinkeye was the urine of a faithful wife. Because urine cannot cure pinkeye, there were probably quite a few wives who had a lot of explaining to do through no fault of their own.

Though Egypt was the medical capital of the world, the Hebrew Bible bears no resemblance to the leading medical opinions of their time. Though they spent several centuries in Egypt, the Bible does not include Egyptian medical practices, especially those involving magic. So how did the Hebrews differ from the Egyptians? First, they treated waste material properly. They were instructed to bury it outside the camp (Deuteronomy 23:12, 13). Second, they were instructed not to touch the dead and to wash themselves with water should they come in contact with a body or carcass (Leviticus 11:24, 23-40; Numbers 19:11-22), which may seem like a common sense approach today. But the ancient world had no concept of germ theory and could not identify harmful microscopic organisms. Third, they made use of quarantine for what today would be known as communicable diseases, such as leprosy (cf. Leviticus 13:45, 46). Finally, dietary restrictions of the Mosaic Law generally provided food that was much cleaner and healthier for individual health. For instance, animals that chew the cud are often healthier than those that do not (cf. Leviticus 11:1-3), and fish with fins and scales are often cleaner than bottom-dwelling marine animals that don't have them (cf. Deuteronomy 14:9). Eating improperly cooked pork is responsible for a number of diseases because pigs are scavengers who can and do consume disease- and bacteria-laden carcasses of other animals. Israelites were not to eat carrion, which could contain bacteria and disease (Leviticus 11:39, 40).

Leprosy is another case of the miraculous foresight contained in the Bible. Until Dr. Armauer Hansen discovered in 1873 that the disease was bacteriological, medical experts believed that leprosy was caused by anything from spicy food to spoiled fish. Some even thought it was because of a certain conjunction of the planets. In Egypt, magical cures were invoked that supposedly counteracted the efforts of demonic powers causing the disease. The biblical remedy sounds very much like modern methods of quarantine. Leviticus 13:46 says, "He shall remain unclean as long as he has the disease [leprosy]. He is unclean. He shall live alone. His dwelling shall be outside the camp." Additionally, the leper was to cover his mouth and warn those who came near him (v. 45). Covering the mouth prohibited transmission of the disease by the tiny droplets of saliva produced during speech. There was no possible way of the Israelites knowing this detail.

In Vienna, Austria in the mid-1800s, Dr. Ignaz Semmelweis became concerned with the high numbers of deaths among pregnant women. One out of six admitted to the hospital died, diagnosed with a mysterious illness called "labor fever." Semmelweis noted that doctors performed autopsies prior to examining the pregnant women, usually without washing their hands. When Semmelweis demanded that they sanitize their hands in chlorinated water before conducting their examinations, the death rate dropped dramatically. The doctors were the cause for all the fatalities, unknowingly spreading disease from corpses to living patients. Semmelweis' isolation of the dead from the living is found millennia earlier in the Bible, where it says, "Whoever touches the dead body of any person shall be unclean seven days" (Num. 19:11). Anyone quarantined would have to wash before rejoining the community.

The marvelous teaching of the Old Testament on health concerns is inexplicable when one examines the ancient evidence. The instructions of the law are consistent with knowledge of advanced hygiene and even germ theory inaccessible to ancient man.

How Do We Know We Have the Right Books?

Christians are familiar with the Gospels of Matthew, Mark, Luke, and John, but some scholars are boldly stating that gospels such as Thomas, Peter, and Judas—among others—should be considered Christian as well. With the discoveries of other gospels, some Christians wonder if they have the correct books in their Bibles. Are these extrabiblical books really inspired, or are they nothing more than writing of an ordinary sort?

The mark of inspiration was one key to admitting books into the New Testament canon. In addition to the theological unity of the prospective books with established Scripture, another important mark was the inspiration of the authors. There were several other books that some in the early church thought should be in the Bible, such as the *Gospel of Barnabas*, the *Didache*, and the *Shepherd of Hermas*. Members of the early church believed these books were helpful, and various authorities recommended them for reading. Ultimately, they were rejected in the end because although they were written very early, they were judged to have been authored by uninspired men.

The books of the Bible were considered authoritative. It is often alleged that the Old Testament was not compiled until the Jewish council at Jamnia in AD 90, and that the New Testament was not compiled until the Council of Nicea in AD 325. Both are incorrect. For example, seventy five years after Jeremiah prophesied, Daniel regarded his prophecy as the "word of the LORD" (Daniel 9:2). Similarly, even New Testament authors recognized the writings of other authors of books of the Bible as inspired Scripture (1 Timothy 5:18; 2 Peter 3:16).

The church spent a considerable amount of time weeding out other books. One such case is the *Gospel of Peter*, which is known from a quotation in the work of the church historian Eusebius (c. 263-339). In the early second century, a bishop of Antioch named Serapion approved the *Gospel of Peter* for use in the local church, thinking Peter authored the book. When it was later discovered to have several Gnostic passages, he immediately rejected its use in the churches. The early church leaders, who did not approve of Gnosticism or any other heretical system of teaching or the documents in which such heresy was detected, mirrored Serapion's attitude.

Another obvious case of such a book is the famous *Gospel of Thomas*. Discovered at Nag Hammadi in 1947, the gospel includes 114 sayings of Jesus. It is called a "sayings-only" gospel because there is no story of Jesus' birth, miracles, crucifixion, or resurrection. On one occasion in the gospel, Peter gets upset because Jesus shows affection to Mary Magdalene. Jesus tells him to stand down, because she is at a disadvantage due to her gender. She cannot have salvation unless Christ first turns her into a male (saying 72).

This misogynistic view of women is one thing that very frequently divides divinely revealed religion from that manufactured by human beings. The opening chapters of Genesis are clear that women are of equal worth and equal value as men. The New Testament agrees here, that women are no less children of God than men (Galatians 3:26-29). Although men and women may have different roles, there is no superior or inferior. The text of Genesis makes it clear that man and woman are completed by the other, and one cannot claim inherent superiority or greater value. Both are made in the image of God.

Other religions put women in a much different place. The ancient Greeks believed that the first humans were all male and that the first woman, Pandora, was responsible for unleashing all of the world's evils. Judaism veered away from the Hebrew Bible toward a pattern of male superiority, as did Islam. The horrors of Sharia law on the extreme end of the spectrum demonstrate the masculine dominance in Islam, where women may be stoned to death for being seen with a non related male in public. Sadly, even Christianity has its share of men who have abused their spiritual leadership and used it to bludgeon their wives into submission, in stark contrast to clear biblical teaching.

Conclusion

The evidence for the inspiration of the Bible is compelling because there is so little room for alternative interpretations. It is one thing to have a book that is consistent. It is another to have a book written by a staff of authors separated by hundreds of years and thousands of miles living in radically different cultures who do not contradict one another. Many books throughout human history contain a great deal of folk wisdom concerning medical knowledge, but it is something else entirely to have a book that shows what could almost be called foreknowledge of medical practice that would not be discovered for thousands of years.

There are a number of features in the Bible that would be considered mysterious oddities if found in other books written by human beings. The fact that the Bible has a divine Author is not a far-fetched idea. Looking at some of the evidence, this appears to be the best explanation for the data at hand. Homer never talked about advanced medicine. The Egyptians were terribly inconsistent in their religious beliefs. To propose a sufficient theory to explain the uniqueness of the Bible would require a level of imagination that borders on the miraculous. The real explanation is far, far simpler. The God of the universe simply chose to write a book telling us about Himself.

Truth 10

Christianity Is Unique

Christianity has a paradoxical nature. Of all the world's religions, it is perhaps the most familiar but least understood. The importance of the Christian faith in shaping the world and culture in which we live is nothing short of monumental. It has inspired the world's greatest artists and composers and given hope to hundreds of millions of people. Despite being attacked by critics the world over and declared intellectually dead, Christianity continues to thrive and grow. Nearly every nation in the world has some percentage of people in its population who declare themselves believers in the God of the Bible. Despite its popularity, it continually suffers a lack of understanding, if not misunderstanding.

Twenty-first century America is a culture immersed in, but systemically ignorant of, religion. The average person's knowledge of professional sports, celebrities, fashion, or any aspect of the media will invariably outstrip their knowledge of religion in general and Christianity in particular. While the early days of American education often featured school curricula that made frequent references to the Bible, modern times are much different. If a person has a single course in college on world religions or an introduction to philosophy, they make up an elite minority.

It is no wonder why religion—along with politics—is a topic any good dinner host avoids like the plague. Discussions of religion invariably feature dissuasive arguments supported by little evidence and a great deal of bombast. For this very reason, those who are undaunted by deep philosophical subjects frequently transform into Houdini-like escape artists once the subject of religion is broached.

Part of our problem in America is the fact that we are immersed in a culture grounded in Judeo-Christian beliefs; yet for all our familiarity we are profoundly ignorant of it. As some have put it, if we could compare the average person's knowledge of religion to a body of water, we would have a swimming pool three miles wide and one inch deep. This ignorance of religion allows for a great deal of distortion not only of Christianity but of other religions as well. In our modern world of diversity and tolerance, it is quite common to hear "religions are all after the same thing."

How unique is Christianity? Is it really all about sincerity as many people claim? Or does the teaching of the Bible stand unique to the other purported holy books of world religion?

The Similarity and Uniqueness of Ancient Israel

Any discussion of the uniqueness of Christianity must begin with ancient Israel. After all, Christianity emerged from and was heavily influenced by Judaism. This is not surprising because the Bible itself shows a continuity between the Old and New Testaments. With Christ's arrival on Earth, the kingdom of God is expanded to include the entire world, even though it was first revealed to the Jews. It is the earliest points of revelation that we will concern ourselves with now.

After the birth of archaeology in the 1700s, scholars witnessed an explosion of new information about the Bible. As the languages of the ancient Near East were deciphered and thousands of new texts translated, new and surprising information about the ancient world came to light. Along with this wealth of new information, scholars have found a number of distinctive elements of Israelite religion that set it apart from the larger empires such as Egypt, Assyria, and Babylon as well as the surrounding Canaanite population in ancient Palestine. First, Israel had a set of dietary laws that is observable in the archaeological record. There are virtually no pig bones in the earliest Israelite settlements in the Judean highlands dating back to 1200-1100 BC. In some places where Philistine cities were in close proximity, archaeologists have found pig bones but none in adjacent Israelite territory.

Second, Israel was forbidden to engage in a number of common religious practices such as human sacrifice, the use of divination or astrology (Deuteronomy 4:19; 18:9-12; 1 Corinthians 6:9, 10; Galatians 5:20, 21) and contacting the dead through a medium or spiritualist. They were to make no idols and were forbidden to make altars of shaped stones. Contrary to the Mosaic Law, Israelites did make idols of a Canaanite goddess, perhaps Asherah. However, there are no depictions of Yahweh found anywhere in Israel. While the Israelites did not depict God like other people depicted their deities, they did fail in turning to polytheism. But it is important to note that despite the people's failures the Bible does take a very different stance when it comes to the exclusive monotheistic worship of God.

Third, there are important theological elements in the Bible. It has been noted in many times and places that greater civilizations influence smaller ones, but this is not the case with Israel's beliefs about God. He is not part of creation, and He is not dependent upon any material thing. God is self-existent and serves as the standard for power and moral rightness. This is unlike other gods who were limited in power and influence and were also petty, vindictive, and morally corrupt. There are even suggestions in Greek literature that humanity was nobler than the gods.

Fourth, the relationship that Israel had with Yahweh was much different than other people's relationships to their mythical gods. In the Bible, man is the pinnacle of God's creative activity and bears His image. God designs man to have a relationship with Him. Other gods created their people as slaves to do the divine dirty work, and the gods were often capricious and destructive. They rarely heard prayers, and man often lived in fear of them.

One Religion Among Many?

Christians have seen one challenge after another mounted against the faith. In the nineteenth century, scholars began applying the ideas of evolution to the study of religion. The resulting model teaches that man started out in animism, believing in animate forces that lived within inanimate objects. He moved on to spiritism, in which he conceives of invisible spirits that inhabit the world beside him. Next came polytheism, the concept of many manlike gods that inhabit the world. Naturally, this would move further still to monotheism, the belief in one god. Finally, the truly enlightened person would simply continue toward atheism. Godlessness was seen as the pinnacle of human evolution of thought and the abandonment of primitive unscientific beliefs. This is still commonly believed, although contradictory evidence exists.

In the twentieth century scholars set out on a journey to discover the essence of religion. The study of comparative religion sought to identify the basic core of religion, to boil it down to its constituent components. Surely religious truth was found in all religions. Because of this, religion was reduced to its lowest common denominator. They came up with two very general principles: (1) the universal fatherhood of God and (2) the universal brotherhood of man. Because of this, it seemed that all religions were really working toward the same goal.[i] Though religious books, rites, and actions may be different, all religions were the same at heart. Because of this, none could make a claim to exclusive truth since they all shared a common goal.

The two principles were so basic as to include everything but wound up including virtually nothing. These two concepts do not fit a number of religions, including Christianity. Scripture is clear that adoption into the family of God is not a universal phenomenon. Neither is the universal brotherhood of man, which is contingent upon everyone being a child of God, which likewise is impossible (Matthew 7:21-23).

In the last two centuries, Christians have witnessed the dwindling uniqueness of the faith. All world religions are claimed to believe essentially the same thing, the same God just with individual types of expressions, much like the mountain analogy we saw in chapter 1. Between evolution and comparative religion, Christians have found only the narrowest of passages.

The teaching of the Bible is quite different than other world religions, especially where God is concerned. Some religions, like those from the East, are essentially atheistic (Buddhism). Other religions are polytheistic in nature (as in some African religions), while still others are pantheistic, believing God to be present in everything and everyone (Hinduism). Even the great monotheistic faiths of Christianity, Judaism, and Islam—and to a lesser extent, Zoroastrianism—differ among themselves as to who God is. They cannot all be correct because each one makes claims that contradict the others. One cannot believe in both monotheism and polytheism or in the existence and nonexistence of a personal God. One must be right and the rest must be wrong. The question is this: Which one makes the best claims to truth?

Critics claim that the teachings of Jesus were really nothing new among the religions of the world. Jesus and the Buddha are often compared because their teachings share similarities at many points. Some have gone so far as to say that Jesus borrowed from the Buddha. However, if we compared the teachings of the great sages of history, we would no doubt find many similarities regardless of which teachers were being examined. Sages often find ready audiences because they appeal to universal principles that all people wonder about, such as the reason for evil, the purpose of suffering and the ultimate destiny of the human soul.

Yet there are stunning distinctions between Jesus and other great teachers of the world. Confucius was a great sage, but Jesus is the truth (John 14:6). The Buddha pointed toward the way, but Jesus is the way. Muhammad could raise the sword, but only Jesus could raise the dead (John 11:38-44).

A final consideration is that there are only so many ways to express religious concepts. A point often missed by Christianity's critics is that people look and long for similar things. It is simply part of the human condition. The universality of humanity's need for love, acceptance, freedom, and enablement does not provide sufficient grounds for declaring any religion wrong. Some people may invent a deity who will provide for these things, but that says absolutely nothing about whether such a deity exists. All it says is that humans have basic wants and needs that find expression in religion. One could argue further that the existence of those needs legitimates religion, specifically Christianity once the whole body of evidence is considered.

Lost Gospels and Secret Scriptures

The uniqueness of the Christian faith and the Scripture upon which it is based is a point that has come under assault in the last few centuries. More modern attacks, however, are much more intense. One such criticism is that there are many different kinds of Christianity. Rather than being a faith delivered once and for all (Jude 3) in its completeness, some scholars would argue a very different view. In the minds of some, Christianity as we know it today is just the version that won out in the secret wars over doctrine that took place in the first few centuries of the church's existence.

Members of the Jesus Seminar such as Karen King and Elaine Pagels, as well as textual scholar Bart Ehrman, have argued that there were many different kinds of Christianity in the three or four centuries after Jesus' death, each with sacred books intentionally excluded from the Bible. Their evidence for this claim is one of the greatest archaeological discoveries of the twentieth century. A small cache of documents known as the Nag Hammadi Library was found in 1947 near the village of Nag Hammadi, Egypt. These documents were bound in twelve codices (books) with an additional document in leaf form. This discovery was monumental for Christian studies and would perhaps be considered the greatest single discovery of the last century if it had not been overshadowed by the discovery of the Dead Sea Scrolls two years later in 1949.

The Nag Hammadi library contains a number of gospels, none of which made it into the New Testament. These include the *Gospel of Philip* and the *Gospel of Thomas*, as well as the *Gospel of Truth* and the *Gospel of the Egyptians*. In all, more than fifty gospels besides those found in the New Testament are known from various sources. Matthew, Mark, Luke, and John are familiar names, but others such as Thomas, Peter, and Judas have made themselves known. They also have different messages and emphases. Some even argue that a couple of them belong in the New Testament. According to some scholars, such as Elaine Pagels and other members of the Jesus Seminar, works such as the *Gospel of Thomas* and the *Gospel of Peter* should be included in the New Testament. According to Pagels, Thomas was originally one of the four Gospels, until John booted it out some time in the second century. The question remains: Are these gospels worthy of consideration for inclusion into the New Testament?

The problem with accepting the various gospels that have been uncovered in the last few decades is that they were never accepted by the early church. Not only were they excluded, they were denounced. They are frequently labeled "the lost gospels" by modern revisionists, but the truth is they were never lost. Scribes only copied documents that people wanted. It was very expensive and time consuming because the printing press would not exist until its invention by Johannes Gutenberg in the mid-1400s. The books that were popular, which included the New Testament, were copied. Those that were less popular fell by the wayside. They were claimed by time not out of a crusade to demolish any competing viewpoints but out of simple disuse. They were not lost. They were unused.

We know from early Christian sources that other gospels were barred from use by churches. Origen denounced the extra gospels in his *Homily on Luke 1:11*.

> I know a certain gospel which is called "The Gospel according to Thomas" and a "Gospel according to Matthias," and many others have we read—lest we should in any way be considered ignorant because of those who imagine that they possess some knowledge if they are acquainted with these. Nevertheless, among all these we have approved solely what the Church has recognized, which is that only the four Gospels should be accepted.[ii]

While the "lost gospels" are frequently touted as "alternative histories," the early church condemned them. Further, they show a significant difference with every other book in the Bible. Their non-Christian origin is betrayed by their inclusion of Greek philosophical concepts and reinterpretations of Scripture; most importantly the wholesale reinvention of God and of the creation story of Genesis. The lost gospels are nothing more than Gnostic, pseudo-Christian writings that went against the clear teaching of Jesus and the apostles.

Who Are My People?

The uniqueness of Christianity is easily seen in the lives of people. The message of the Bible is for everyone, regardless of race, color, or creed. If we were to step back into the first century, things would be quite different than what we find in modern society. Gone would be the days of equality for many social groups.

Let's step back and look at Jesus' attitude toward others through His teachings. In Luke 10:25-37, Jesus tells the parable of a good

Samaritan, although in His day there was no such thing according to His fellow Jews. Samaritans weren't good; they were bad. Very bad. According to the Babylonian Talmud the death penalty did not apply to a Jew who murdered a Samaritan. The Mishnah says that eating bread baked by a Samaritan was no better than eating pork. Violence escalated between the Jews and Samaritans in the couple of centuries before Christ. In the eyes of His Jewish audience, Jesus chose the worst possible hero for His story. Of course, this makes the Samaritan the best possible choice, because Jesus was trying to teach these people that human beings shouldn't be put into classes defined by worth.

Jesus also takes a moment to speak to a Samaritan woman with a reputation for getting around in John 4. She had three strikes against her. She was (1) female, (2) a Samaritan, and (3) less than pure. No self-respecting Jewish male would have given her a second glance. Even Jesus' disciples are surprised when they catch up with Him. But Jesus sees a person in need of truth. For Him, the need to hear the truth trumps manmade social mores.

Finally, Jesus uses children to rebuke his own disciples (Matthew 19:13-15). This must have stunned them. Here were men who had heard the teachings of Jesus and experienced Him firsthand. And He pulls a couple of little kids out of the crowd and tells His trusty sidekicks that they need to be like children? Jesus was probably getting at the fact that children seem to have an implicit level of trust of older adults and especially parents. Couldn't Jesus have used a better example? Not with a worldview that sees all human beings are equally valuable.

The equal value of people is a virtue that goes unnoticed all too often in the Bible. World history is full of the stronger oppressing the weaker, and this has manifested itself by putting women into a secondary class of value to men. Yet we do not find that in the Bible. In Genesis 2 we see that woman is created with love and care in a fashion that has artistic overtones. It is almost as if God's creation is incomplete until woman is created. She is the final brush stroke on the divine masterpiece. Unfortunately, God's people were influenced more by the surrounding culture than by His messengers.

Other cultures held women in very low esteem. According to the Greek writer Hesiod, women nagged too much and couldn't contribute to their own upkeep. Additionally, in his most famous work, the *Theogony*, the first human beings were men. Only later does the first woman appear. Pandora by name, she is given a box full of the world's ills for safekeeping. One day curiosity gets the best of her and she opens the box, letting all the evils of the world escape. According to this Greek myth, all the world's evils are the result of a foolish and overly inquisitive female.

The beauty of the Bible is seen in the fact that the harsh judgments and devaluation of the individual is not found in Scripture. While Paul is often charged with misogyny, the apostle makes it clear that all people, regardless of gender, ethnicity, or social standing can be heirs of God (Galatians 3:26-29).

Grace is perhaps the one defining characteristic of Christianity that sets it apart from other world religions. The Buddhist travels the eight-fold path; the Hindu must escape the cycle of karma; Judaism must keep to the covenant; the Muslim must also keep to Islamic law. Each system offers a way to earn one's way to the ultimate goal. The Christian cannot earn his way into the presence of God. That ticket was purchased two thousand years ago.

Christianity's uniqueness is a curious thing. The faith is distinctive because its Scriptures are also distinctive. This fact is largely unrecognized, and often criticized. Skeptics like to say that the Bible didn't just "drop out of the heavens." Apart from the fact that no Christian actually believes that the Bible fell from the clouds one day, it does bring up a very important question about who wrote it. It had to come from somewhere. That's our next question.

Truth 11

Early Christians Were Not Plagiarists

Plagiarism is one of the gravest academic offenses one can commit. It is stealing and taking credit for another person's intellectual property. A journalist who plagiarizes a source, even unintentionally, can expect to suffer suspension or even termination. The same goes for anyone in academia. Even an innocent mistake can be enough to ruin a scholar's reputation.

The literary crime of plagiarism is the offense of which the New Testament authors are guilty according to some critics. The biblical writers simply stole ideas from pagan religions and incorporated them into their stories about Jesus. This includes not only particular teachings and beliefs but larger theological matters as well. Some will say that even Jesus is nothing more than a pagan deity. According to one bumper sticker, "Christianity has pagan DNA."

The great worldwide rumor mill known as the Internet doesn't help matters much. One can expect nearly every atheistic website on the Internet to include something about early Christians stealing the intellectual property of older and more established religions. While some critics simply deny the originality of Christian claims, others paint a very different portrait of the faith. The more hostile critics actively accuse Christians of stealing from other religions, then denying the theft ever took place. They claim Christianity is dishonest, if not criminal.

Some Christians will dismiss these allegations, choosing to favor the Bible over agenda-driven media hounds. Other Christians inevitably react with fear, allowing the seeds of doubt to creep in and take root. In what quickly becomes a dark night of the soul, they ask themselves, "Is this true? And if so, is my faith misplaced?" which leads to the unavoidable question, "Does God really exist?"

Old-Time Religion

It is increasingly popular among the membership of the lunatic fringe to claim Jesus and the Christian faith are little more than whitewashed paganism. Early Christian writers essentially took myths from the religions of ancient Greece, Rome, Phrygia, Persia, Egypt, Syria, and others, and gave them a fresh face, calling it "Jesus." The Bible is a book of plagiarized myths, and Jesus is a copycat Christ.

The borrowing runs deep according to critics. Jesus shares many features with these other pagan gods, including birth on December 25; visited by three wise men from the East; popular teachers, disciples; public baptism and ministry beginning at age thirty, which included performing miracles such as healing the sick and walking on water. Later, they were betrayed, crucified, buried for three days, and resurrected. From start to finish, Jesus is claimed to be nothing more than a pagan god *redux*.

Self-proclaimed scholars Timothy Freke and Peter Gandy ask, "Why should we consider the stories of Osiris, Dionysus, Adonis, Attis, Mithras, and other Pagan Mystery saviors as fables, yet come across essentially the same story told in a Jewish context and believe it to be the biography of a carpenter from Bethlehem?"[i] Tom

Harpur, a former Anglican priest, says, "Not one single doctrine, rite, tenet, or usage in Christianity was in reality a fresh contribution to the world."[ii] According to Harpur and his forebears Gerald Massey (1828-1907), Godfrey Higgins (1772-1833), and Alvin Boyd Kuhn (1880-1963), Christianity is nothing more than a lightly edited version of Egyptian mythology. So what is the Christian to do? Is the faith really nothing more than an exercise in plagiarism?

Virtually all scholars agree that Christianity does not have pagan DNA. Writers who make that assertion are not experts in any sense of the word and usually have no academic credentials to speak of. In fact, they are so obscure that even prominent New Testament scholars don't know who they are. But we could ask: Even if the proponents of Christian plagiarism aren't scholars, does that automatically invalidate what they say? After all, history is full of amateurs who made significant discoveries of their own despite not having a great deal of expertise. Amateurs can and do make important finds. But we also have to look at the opposite side of the equation. What are the experts saying?

There are plenty of scholars who have spent lifetimes studying the relevant materials. They spend countless hours studying the sources in the original languages. They publish technical works that other scholars can critique. In short, these are people who know as much as anyone in the world. The vast majority dismiss the idea of plagiarism as ridiculous. By way of contrast, let's look at those who argue Christianity is plagiarized. Massey was a poet, Higgins a lawyer. Kuhn was a high school language teacher. Harpur is an agenda-driven journalist. Compare them with scholars, even unbelieving ones, who spend tens of thousands of hours in a lifetime of sober, detailed study. There really is no comparison. There is almost no mention of them in scholarly literature because the experts choose not to waste their time refuting crackpot conspiracy theories.

When we read the Gospels, we find that their authors are very concerned with the important questions: who, what, when, and where. This is quite unlike myth, which has little concern for locating events in actual history. Even pagans rarely believed that their own myths actually happened in real time and space. The Gospels are radically different, expecting their readers to take them as factual accounts. The difference is because of the fact that myth is concerned primarily with stories of the gods. The Gospels are concerned with what really happened during the life of Christ.

The view that the Gospels are myth comes in part from the "history of religions school" in the mid-nineteenth century. It sought to tie religions together, claiming that nothing new is really ever introduced, only reworked from another source. The idea that the biblical authors used ideas found in pagan sources—especially the Greek mystery religions—stands fully in line with this type of reasoning. Although the approach was totally debunked by the mid-twentieth century, its leftovers are still hanging around in the popular consciousness. In their book *Reinventing Jesus*, New Testament scholars Komoszewski, Sawyer, and Wallace call this type of approach "junk food for the mind—a pseudointellectual meal that is as easy to swallow as it is devoid of substance."[iii] Sadly, half a century after the claims were refuted, they persist in popular criticism.

One of the most important considerations when resolving this issue is this: What was the relationship of the Christian authors to paganism? If the charge of plagiarism is to stick, it must correctly represent the evidence we have on hand. In most cases, we find out that most of the evidence connecting Christianity to the mystery religions comes from the second century and later. Even some of the most radical critics of the Bible admit that the New Testament was composed in the first century, meaning that the ideas simply did not exist for the biblical authors to steal. There is a possibility that the ideas existed much sooner and just didn't leave any evidence, but that is pure speculation. We must work from the evidence at hand, not from conjecture. Some suggest that the other religions may have been influenced by Christianity.

Another important factor to investigate is what is the nature of the parallels? Is there obvious borrowing, or is the similarity coincidental? Or is the similarity manufactured by the critic? There are some parallels between Christianity and mystery religions that quickly evaporate once we do some digging. For instance, both Christianity and the mystery religions featured a God or gods who offered salvation (*soteria*). On the surface, it sounds like a lock for borrowing on the part of the biblical authors. However, the kind of salvation offered was radically different. The mystery religions offered salvation in the form of independence from the blind power of fate. Christianity offers salvation from sin and deliverance from the power of death (Romans 5:20, 21; 6:23). The two could hardly be more different.

In some cases, similarity can be manufactured. In this case, the critic, whether layman or scholar, simply describes features of Greek religion using Christian language, so it makes the two appear much more similar than they really are. One example is the *taurobolium* (sacrifice of a bull) in the Mithraic Mysteries. Mithras was a Persian deity around whom a mystery religion developed. An initiate into the mysteries would stand in a pit. Above him was a young bull whose throat was slit. The gore would wash over the initiate covering him entirely. I had one professor who described the process and echoed the old hymn, saying, "It's like the person was being 'washed in the blood.'" In reality, the practice had nothing to do with baptism or washing away sin, as the professor implied. The first evidence of the *taurobolium* comes from a century after the apostle Paul, making it impossible for the New Testament writers to have borrowed anything from this practice. The only connections between the *taurobolium* and Christ's crucifixion are due to chronological errors on the part of modern writers.

Finally, we must ask if the ideas present in Christianity and the mystery religions are similar because of borrowing, or if it is something much simpler, like the expression of a common idea. Religions in general are often concerned with similar things. The human condition is universal, and religion can and does arise to meet the needs that all human beings face. Religion helps meet a person's need for acceptance and strength in the face of adversity. It also serves as a source of love and care. In some cases, it acts as a goad to a higher ethic of personal and professional behavior. Many religions—including Christianity—do all of these things. For instance, it should be of no surprise that the Buddha and Jesus say things that sound similar at times. Both were wise men who addressed the needs of others. It just so happens that Jesus was also God incarnate. It does not mean that they have borrowed from one another. Similarity does not equal dependency.

On a final note, it is sometimes brought out that Justin Martyr (c. AD 100-164) discussed parallels between Jesus and other mythological figures, such as the Greek hero Perseus. In a letter to the Roman emperor he argues that the Romans have no need to persecute Christians because they aren't all that different from their pagan neighbors. The catch? Justin is trying to stave off Roman persecution. If the Christians aren't that different from the pagans, then there should be no need for the Romans to persecute the Christians. Justin didn't really do his homework though. The connections between Christ and other pagan figures aren't very good. While his argument was noble in its intent, it was no more successful than critics who argue the church ripped off the pagan religions.

Signs and Wonders: Mythical, Magical, or Miraculous?

One of the easiest ways to claim Christianity is a rip-off is to describe other myths using Christian language. Unfortunately, this is done quite often and appears to be quite convincing if taken at face value. Here's how it works: a pagan god is called a "savior" and is claimed to have been crucified and resurrected. Never mind that the god isn't a savior, and wasn't crucified or resurrected. That's not the point—the point is to sound convincing, and authors claiming to be scholars exercise no caution, responsibility, or objectivity in making these imaginary connections between Christian faith and

Early Christians Were Not Plagiarists

other religions. As Princeton Theological Seminary Professor Bruce Metzger once put it, "It goes without saying that alleged parallels which are discovered ... evaporate when they are confronted with the original texts. In a word, one must beware of what have been called, 'parallels made plausible by selective description.' "[iv]

The virgin birth appears to be something unique to Christianity. No divine figure in the ancient world was virgin born, as much as critics try to make it appear otherwise. The ancients did not have a concept of nonsexual reproduction. Although modern critics claim that the virgin birth is found in other mystery religions, there is one important consideration to make from one of Christianity's earliest critics. Celsus was a second-century opponent of Christianity. The early church father Origen wrote *Contra Celsum*, in which he addressed Celsus' criticisms. Celsus' work is no longer extant (in existence), but Origen preserves some of his arguments while in the process of refuting them. In one place, Origen says that Celsus said Jesus invented His virgin birth and was instead illegitimate. If the virgin birth was so common among Greek religion, why didn't Celsus say that Jesus stole the idea from other sources? It would be much more devastating to make that argument than claim, with no support, that Jesus simply invented the idea.

Some say that crucifixion is nothing new. In reality, it is. The gods Osiris of Egypt and Attis of Phrygia are claimed to have been crucified. Actually, Osris dies by being drowned in a wooden box, and Attis wounds himself and dies underneath a tree. The only similarity these deaths have with Roman crucifixion is that something made of wood is in the vicinity, which, of course, is really no similarity at all.

Likewise, there are no true resurrection experiences found in other religions. Many figures are offered as examples, but none are actually resurrected. The closest example would be Osiris in ancient Egypt. He is drowned by his brother Seth, and later dismembered and the pieces scattered over the land. His wife Isis gathers them together and brings him to life by magic, but Osiris remains as ruler of the underworld. His death seems to be the first case of mummification, (which has no parallel outside of ancient Egyptian religion), and being the lord of the dead doesn't count as true resurrection. While Osiris remains in the abode of the dead, the New Testament explicitly states that Christ ascended to glory.

First-Century Magic Men

Granted that Jesus was a real person (as we saw in chapter 6), was He nothing more than that? What about the miracle stories? In an age where scientific qualification reigns supreme, this is an important question to ask. Critics frequently point to miracle stories highlighting other figures from antiquity. Whether it is something like resurrection or something less monumental like healing, curing demonic possession, or walking on water, there is no shortage of accusations from skeptics and critics.

Jesus is supposedly a miracle worker like others in the ancient world. One such example is Apollonius of Tyana. He was a popular teacher and found himself in opposition to the Christians in the early second century. Like Jesus, Apollonius' followers credited him with performing miracles, the greatest of which was raising a girl from the dead. Some are quick to point out that Jesus was not alone in His wonder-working routine, but others are just as quick to respond that the ancient evidence suggests that not all of Apollonius' followers believed he performed such great works. Many of his miracles were disputed among his followers. Furthermore, there is virtually no material prior to the third century about him.

The charge of borrowing on the part of the biblical authors where the miracles of Jesus are concerned is hard to prove. Of course that does not stop the critics from claiming it, but it does make it harder. Miracle stories from the ancient world are often outlandish or disproportionately effective. Magic is conspicuously absent from the Bible, despite being a vital feature of every neighboring civilization in the ancient world. This is true not only in the life and ministry of Christ but in the Old Testament also. From the earliest periods of Egyptian and Mesopotamian civilization through the Greco-Roman culture experienced by the apostles, magic was integral to the understanding of how the world worked. Except for the biblical writers that is. Magic is forbidden (Deuteronomy 18:9-12), and everything supernatural is credited to God.

How Do You Respond?

The Bible has seen challenges come and go over the past two thousand years, and it's highly doubtful that anything new could pose an insurmountable challenge to a faith that has withstood millennia of scrutiny and skepticism. The reason why extravagant claims never pan out is because there are sensational in nature. They must be provocative, and authors and filmmakers will often take unnecessary liberties with the facts in order to make their productions more exciting. You can be guaranteed that scholars will soon rebut the nonspecialists. In several years, such productions will be forgotten in spite of the sensation they cause, primarily because they don't stick with the facts.

The systemic religious illiteracy of our culture is largely to blame for the criticisms that Christianity is just a baptized version of ancient mythology. In order to expose the fallacies of critical claims, careful analysis is a must. This means getting behind the reasons why a documentary is made or an article is written. Some Christians will glibly say, "They're just in it for the money." That may be true in part, especially since controversy makes a good incentive for garnering advertising dollars. But there are deeper and more meaningful ways to get at the errors found in such offerings. What is the worldview of the critic, and why are those charges being made? Virtually all critics of the Bible embrace a naturalistic philosophy—if it can't be detected with the five senses, then it doesn't exist. This presupposition is intellectually arrogant, however, and is usually only the starting point. Other productions and articles are driven by bias, so evidence is manipulated in order to confirm already-held conclusions. Objectivity is often a mask, which leads us to ask a number of important questions. Does the author appeal to evidence, and is he interpreting that evidence correctly? Are there any unfounded assumptions in the work? How well does the evidence support the author's conclusions? Does the argument contain any logical fallacies? Is the work geared more toward persuasion than explanation?

Another important question to ask is, "How do the scholars respond?" Many qualified biblical experts frequently denounce media productions for the same reasons we have just mentioned. In the case of the *Lost Tomb of Jesus*, scholars came out of the woodwork to denounce the show, and most of them were unbelievers. In the case of *Zeitgeist, the Movie*, several atheists heavily criticized the production in Internet websites because it was full of bad arguments, and they were afraid that an atheist using those arguments against Christians would be made to look foolish. The world is full of scholars who believe that the Bible is the inspired Word of God and are not afraid to demolish bad arguments against it.

Finally, it is important to remain cool and collected in the face of challenges. The Bible is no paper tiger. It has withstood the heaviest assaults of history's most brilliant critics, yet it remains the world's most important book today. Hundreds of millions still look to it as the Word of God. It is the Bible's resiliency that gives the believer confidence that any challenge produced will be met with adequate explanation. It has done so for two millennia, and shows no signs of stopping anytime soon.

Truth 12

God Loves Sinners

Street preachers are an interesting lot. They have to be admired for their boldness. When I was in high school, I passed one of these men one day at the front of a mall in downtown Nashville. He was passionately reading from the Bible, preaching his heart out to anyone who would listen. I remember thinking, "How effective is he? Is he really accomplishing anything?" My suspicions were confirmed when I looked around. People walked past him oblivious. They appeared to be going about their business as usual, almost as if he didn't exist.

One night on the Fourth of July a few years later, I was walking down the sidewalk after a brilliant fireworks display. I saw a man standing up on a low wall, waving his arms and shouting to the passersby. As I drew closer, I began picking up some of what he was saying. "Do you know where you're going when you die?" He shouted as the pedestrians passed by, most of them giving little credence to this sidewalk evangelist. When I got close to him, he looked me in the eye and asked the same question. "Do you know where you're going when you die?" I replied, "Yeah, I'm going to heaven, man!" He didn't respond. I looked into his glazed-over eyes and saw a man on autopilot. A split second later he looked away and repeated his question to the next face in the crowd.

This young man, apparently well meaning, wasn't really interested in hearing anyone's response. His message was pretty simple: If you aren't a Christian, you're going to hell—the typical fire and brimstone sermon condensed into a sound byte format. I admired him for his unashamed presentation of the gospel but also questioned the choice of style in that presentation. Peter makes it clear that all Christians are to be ready to provide a sound defense for why they believe what they believe but that the defense should also stem from "good behavior in Christ" (1 Peter 3:15; 2 Peter 3:15, 16). While I admired this tenacious young man for his spirit, his lack of interest in a response from his hearers probably sounded very hollow to most of the crowd.

Glorious Failure

King David is perhaps one of the most beloved persons in Scripture. Some have called him "David the Great," which calls to mind all the other great leaders of history who also bore that eponym. We might think of Alexander the Great, who conquered the Persian Empire before turning thirty. Clocking in at just under a decade, the Macedonian prince masterminded a lightning-fast military campaign that bulldozed the Persian Empire—the world's largest at the time. We could think of Ramesses the Great, one of ancient Egypt's greatest pharaohs, whose likeness still graces Egyptian currency. Russian rulers Peter and Catherine the Great both guided Russia into a powerful empire that was remarkably European and just as powerful.

David is similar to other great rulers in history. He was a great military leader, poet, musician, and administrator. That his kingdom was smaller than, say, that of Alexander the Great doesn't necessarily make his accomplishments any less grand. People seemed to be naturally drawn to him. His daring and tenacity are the stuff of legend. So is his faith—and his sin.

God Loves Sinners

The Bible consistently presents a picture of the saints "warts and all." This is especially true for the patriarchs. Abraham, the father of the faith, twice lies to save his own skin. His son Isaac does the same. Jacob is a cheat, and his first four sons are anything but sterling examples of moral behavior. Reuben (incest), Levi and Simeon (murder), and Judah (adultery) have more than their fair share of moral failures. The same goes for David. He leads a crack corps of Philistine brigands, threatens to kill a man for refusing him hospitality, and lies to his Philistine overlord about decimating Philistine villages. But that's not the worst of it.

David's troubles began when he solidified his position as the king of Israel. In 2 Samuel 11:1, the text notes, "In the spring of the year, the time when kings go out to battle ... David remained at Jerusalem." The scene immediately turns to the palace. Here is David, the great warrior, at home. His troops are out on the battlefield, but he stays put. It is often said that the idle mind is the devil's playground. The king's sumptuous palace is no mere playground. It's Disney World.

Taking a leisurely stroll on the rooftop of his palace, David spies a beautiful woman bathing. Rather than turning his head, he leans in for a closer look. He wants to know who this woman is. He is told that she is Bathsheba, the wife of Uriah the Hittite. Another man's wife? No matter. Kings get whatever they want. It's good to be the king.

After spending the night together, Bathsheba is sent away in the morning. David's one-night stand is over, or so he thinks. Bathsheba soon discovers that she is pregnant. Frantically, David pulls her husband Uriah in from the battlefield and schemes to get him to go home to his wife. Uriah, a Gentile who is more faithful that the Hebrew monarch himself, refuses to go home even after David gets him drunk. His schemes fail, and David resorts to more extreme measures.

For the record, David has now committed one crime punishable by death under the law and is conspiring to commit a second. Both adultery (Deuteronomy 22:23, 24) and murder (Exodus 21:12) are capital crimes. The only hope he has is to keep it a secret. Despite

David's covert machinations, the palace seems to be buzzing with messengers. Servants had to sneak Bathsheba back to her house. Messengers race between David and Joab right and left to work out the details of the murder plot. Like so many conspiracies, the more involved the scheme, the more there are who know about what is supposed to be kept secret. Regardless, the plan is in motion.

We can only imagine what was running through the mind of Uriah on the battlefield that day. In our mind's eye we see him fighting for king and country, loyal to both and willing to forsake neither. His weapon flashes again and again, mowing down the enemy like a buzzsaw. He hears the command to withdraw, but soon finds himself encircled by the opposition. He sees his fellow soldiers retreating out of the corner of his eye and tries to follow them, but his escape is quickly sealed off. A sling stone crashes into his shoulder, shattering it and rendering his arm useless. Despite his handicap, his weapon still finds its mark time and again. Like a caged animal, the mighty man fights with the ferocity of ten.

The enemy closes in. All alone, it is only a matter of time. Uriah's defenses slip for just a moment, and someone hits him from the side. He stumbles and falls in the confusion. His foes pounce. The last image he sees is a warrior standing over him, weapon raised. His last thought is a prayer to Yahweh to safeguard the king he feels he has failed and the wife he is leaving behind. With a swift, merciless stroke, the deed is done.

A messenger brings back a report from the field. Joab's troops suffer staggering losses and David is outraged. The messenger hastily adds one final note, a curious addition that his general reminded him to include: "Uriah the Hittite is dead also" (2 Samuel 11:24). With that tiny piece of information, the king's anger vanishes. David adopts a conciliatory tone. He says, "[T]he sword devours now one and now another" (v. 25). And in some cases, it almost appears as if it can devour secret sin as well. Almost.

The Heart of the King

Not long after, a prophet comes to visit David. Prophets were God's spokesmen, and they usually brought bad news. Scholars have referred to them as the prosecuting attorneys of the covenant because they frequently reminded the people that they have failed to keep their end of the bargain. Israel consistently and persistently failed to keep the covenant and remain faithful to Yahweh. It could range anywhere from religious abuses to social injustice to murder. Prophets weren't always a welcome sight. If one came to knock on your door, it was probably because you did something very, very bad.

Nathan comes to visit David and present him with what appears to be a legal case. Because one of the king's functions includes making legal decisions, it seems altogether appropriate. Nathan relates the sad story of a man whose pet lamb is forcefully taken by a wealthy man who is too cheap to sacrifice one of his own flock to feed a visiting traveler. The lamb was like a daughter to the man, who had raised her from birth and treated her like one of his own children. For any pet lover, this story is nothing short of a heinous crime. That's exactly how David takes it. He thinks back on his days as a shepherd. He protected them and cared for them. At times, the sheep were his only friends in the wilderness. What the rich man had done was no simple theft. It was murder.

The Hebrew monarch shoots straight up from his seat and demands that the offender be hauled before an executioner. Because he did this and had no pity, David is ready to book him for a quick trip to the afterlife. We might be inclined to agree. Nathan has played his part well, so well that David doesn't suspect that he is being told a parable. There are tiny clues scattered in the parable that might have tipped him off, but David doesn't catch them. The most curious thing about David is that he sentences the man to die for stealing a sheep. Theft of livestock is not a capital crime. So why does David overreact? Probably because Nathan's skillfully crafted parable pulls the trigger on David's guilty conscience.

The prophet rebukes his king, a risky move by anyone's estimation. David was a king; Nathan was a mere prophet. David could have made Nathan disappear to keep the lid on his not-so-secret secret. He's already done it once. But we also have to give David the credit he deserves. The Hebrew text is not particularly descriptive, but we can imagine David's horror when he realizes that a prophet—a spokesman for God Himself—has just indicted him for murder. David not only committed two capital crimes, but conspired to cover them up. If it were a modern courtroom, David would have already been begging for a plea bargain.

Why do we bring up David's sin? Very simple. Average people are tempted to think of themselves the way the world sees them. It has been said that our opinions of ourselves are not based on what we think or on what others think, but on what we think others are thinking. We watch the gifted, the super competent and the super talented members of society and then go look in the mirror. What do many of us see? Just an average person. Nothing special. That may be what some human beings see, but it isn't what God sees.

Before creation exists, the omniscient God of the universe knows what is going to happen. Before time He knows He is going to create a wonderful, beautiful world full of marvelous living things. So great are the deep wonders of the universe He is going to create that mankind—the pinnacle of His creative activity—will never be able to fully plumb its depths. Philosophers will spend immeasurable time speculating on the nature of the cosmos. Scientists will spend just as long measuring, examining, and quantifying the sprawling universe. It will be so great that humanity will only be able to gaze up at the starry host in childlike wonder. And greatest of all, God is going to tell people about Himself in a wonderful book.

And for all the beautiful things these people will be able to accomplish as image bearers of God (Genesis 1:26), they will betray Him. They will look at the universe and scoff at the idea that it could be created, chalking it up to chance instead. They will label His book an anthology of lies and fairy tales. They will persecute those who believe in Him. But the gravest offense of all will be their murder of His Son. Jesus, who is co-creator with the Almighty (John 1:3), knows the suffering He will have to endure for a race of beings who will spit in His face, beat Him unmercifully, and finally nail Him to a tree with shame and disgust so great that it will force the Father to turn His head for the only time in their eternal relationship.

And He knows all of this before opening His mouth to utter the words that will cause creation to explode into existence. He proceeds as planned, not because He has to, but because He wants someone to whom He can show His love.

'Fess Up

The Bible teaches that humanity is sinful, pure and simple. Sin was introduced in the Garden of Eden (Genesis 3:6-13), leaving in its wake a sin-stained world into which every human being is born. The evil of sin continues through every human being by the choices we make in rebelling against God (Ephesians 2:1-3). Yet God chooses not to abandon His creation, leaving it to destroy itself. Instead, God sets in motion a plan to redeem not only sinful humanity but the entire universe as well. From the beginning, God knows He will send a redeemer to reconcile sinful humanity to Himself. In doing so, there must be a way for humanity to access God's presence. Since God is perfect, He cannot negotiate His own standards of justice for the sake of personal favoritism. Being omniscient, He cannot ignore sin. There is another way.

Jesus tells His audience that He is "the way, and the truth, and the life. No one comes to the Father except through me" (John 14:6). Jesus comes to earth to preach the message of repentance, establishing Himself as the one true way to regain the access to God that was lost thousands of years ago in the Garden of Eden. No one has truly seen the face of God since that time, but there is a day coming when everyone who adopts the name of Christ will have that privilege.

While the Bible clearly teaches that only those in the proper relationship with Christ will be saved, there are a number of faulty beliefs concerning the afterlife held by people one might consider nominal believers. Some people think that God is obligated to save everyone and that a loving God would never send anyone to hell, ever. Others believe that hell is going to be a sparsely populated place for much the same reason. Still others believe that the barest minimum of commitment is enough to guarantee salvation, even if one turns back to a life of sin later in life.

In some cases, God's standards are manipulated and negotiated so that God becomes more of an enabler. There are many people who attempt to legitimize sinful behavior with the simple words, "I know God wants me to be happy." It is often said in the context of someone who wants to leave his or her spouse for a younger, richer, or better-looking model, but it could well be said about anything. God wants people to be happy, but He also holds them accountable. The two are not mutually exclusive.

Because of sin, we stand in a state of guilt before God. There are several different ways to understand guilt. It can be an important feeling that drives someone to excellence, but it can also be a means of disproportionate self-punishment. We decry injustice when it occurs in the justice system, yet there are thousands, if not millions, punishing themselves with the equivalent of an emotional death sentence for the smallest crimes.

It is equally important to recognize that there are two very different kinds of guilt. The first kind of guilt is objective. This refers to a state of being guilty in a legal sense. If an infraction is committed, then the offender is guilty of violating the law. Every person exists in a state of guilt before God because everyone has sinned (Romans 3:23). It is a universal condition and one that Christ came to earth to address.

The second kind of guilt is subjective. This is when a person is in a state of feeling guilty about something. It is irrelevant whether they have actually done anything wrong—a person may break the law and feel guilt, break the law and feel no guilt, or feel guilty for non-reasons found within his or her own imagination. This kind of guilt has many related ideas: regret, sorrow, disappointment, frustration, or exasperation. A person feeling this kind of guilt mulls over his wrongdoings, replaying his crimes—real or imagined—on a big screen television in his mind.

It is interesting to see that the Bible spends almost no time on subjective guilt. It is virtually nonexistent in Scripture. It is almost as if God is telling His readers, "Don't feel guilty. Acknowledge your sin, pick yourself up, and turn things around." In one sense, we are wasting our time by feeling guilty. As long as we make the effort to avoid committing the same mistakes, we have satisfied that part of God's will. As for our standing before God, our sin is covered by the blood of Christ (Ephesians 2:13). When we appeal to Christ and His finished work on the cross, we may stand before God rightfully in a state of innocence.

Some people feel as if they don't deserve forgiveness. In one poll taken in the 1990s, when individuals were given an exam on how they felt about their spiritual state, four percent believed they were going to hell. What they did or didn't do was inconsequential; they were going to burn no matter what. In a sense it doesn't matter what anyone does, because our salvation cannot be earned or bought. Salvation depends upon a God who became a man and paid our debt so that we could spend eternity with Him. Our destiny was sealed two thousand years ago, but realizing it depends upon the simple choice of whether or not to obey the command of Christ.

See You There

We can see that the evidence begins to make sense when we factor God into the equation. When God is left out, things don't quite add up. We see purpose and design but are told that there is no Designer. We are called to imagine a creation without a Creator. The Bible appears to be remarkably reliable, much more so than any other ancient book, yet without God it is little more than a literary freak of nature. All of these call for an explanation, and without God anyone would be hard pressed to find one that sounds remotely plausible. Once we open up our minds to a worldview that is unrestricted by preconceived biases against the supernatural, it is like a camera coming into focus. The blurs and fuzzy shapes begin to crystallize into comprehensible objects. We see things as they really are.

Part of this worldview includes a sharper focus not only of the natural realm but the spiritual one as well. We begin to see God's grand design with greater clarity. We see that there is purpose and meaning to life. Human beings have an intrinsic value by virtue of our creation in the image of God (Genesis 1:26). Part of being made in God's image involves the possibility of entering into relationships. We see that God has created not because He needs but because He loves.

God's love is demonstrated by the fact that He left His autobiography for us to read. Through it we come to know and understand Him. He is not like the gods of the ancient world, who took little notice of humanity unless one of its members stepped out of line. He invites us to know Him and enter into a relationship with Him. Paul tells us "[W]hile we were still sinners, Christ died for us" (Romans 5:8). Does God love sinners? Yes, He does. Enough to let His Son die for them.

Appendix

New Atheism Isn't New

I hate to break it to you, but everything you've read in this book is wrong. Each chapter is full of twisted facts, misinformation, lies, and revisionist history. God doesn't exist, Christianity is evil, and the right-wing conspiracy wants to set up a theocracy to enslave billions. According to the new atheists, that is.

One of the difficulties facing Christians today that will only grow worse in coming days is the recent injection of a virulent form of atheism into Western culture. This recent development in unbelief is often referred to as "new atheism," although it is poorly named. The only real difference between new atheism and old atheism is the level of hostility. Unbelievers in the twentieth century and before were more calculating and sober in their criticism of the faith. New atheists don't seem to care about fairness or propriety. Their arguments border on the obscene. The most worrisome aspect of this movement is that its loudest proponents seem to care very little about being informed about the subject of their criticism.

Richard Dawkins, Christopher Hitchens, and Sam Harris are three of the most famous militant atheists to hit the scene in the last couple of decades. Their work attracts a great deal of media attention, but their style is crass. They demonstrate a catastrophic failure to understand the religions they oppose and give little evidence that they care about understanding the subject of their criticism. In fact, they often make excuses for not ever making the attempt to learn about Christianity. On the popular level, this often takes the form of, "Why bother wasting your time learning about something that isn't true?" Of course we have to ask, "How did you conclude Christianity is false if you've never taken the time to investigate it?"

A Good, Clean Fight

It usually takes very little effort to find evidence of the virulent hostility of the new atheists. Whether it's calling religious people child abusers, critiquing Christian beliefs as "pig-ignorant," or dismissing any argument before the first word is ever spoken, there is no shortage of criticism of the faith. The criticism of the faith can be found in every media format from bookstore shelves to blogs to video clips on the Internet. You can find everything you ever wanted to know about hostile atheism but were afraid to ask.

Much of the hostility of new atheism is directed toward Christianity. While Islam bears the brunt of charges concerning violence and intolerance, Christianity has the lion's share when it comes to all other areas of consideration. Religions other than those connected with the Judeo-Christian tradition generally get little attention, which is a reflection of the new atheist's postmodern view of tolerance: peace and goodwill toward all, except the Christians.

One of the most absurd criticisms of Christianity is the argument that the faith is guilty of child abuse. In an article in the freethought magazine *Free Inquiry* Richard Dawkins argues that religion is abusive to children and that the "threat of eternal hell is an extreme example of mental abuse."[i] Christopher Hitchens agrees, asking, "How can we ever know how many children had their psychological and physical lives irreparably maimed by the compulsory inculcation of faith?"[ii] As a response to believers intent upon

Appendix: New Atheism Isn't New

giving their children a Christian upbringing, Dawkins asks if it should not be a responsibility of the state to prevent parents from doing so. He asks, "How much do we regard children as being the property of their parents? It's one thing to say people should be free to believe whatever they like, but should they be free to impose their beliefs on their children? Is there something to be said for society stepping in? What about bringing up children to believe manifest falsehoods?"[iii]

What the new atheists do not consider is that there are plenty of atheist training programs in America. At Camp Quest, children are taught how to be "freethinkers" unbound by all religious creeds and dogmas. Teaching tools like the Invisible Pink Unicorn and the Flying Spaghetti Monster are used to prove that God does not exist. It probably hasn't ever crossed their minds that it is contradictory to teach children how to think for themselves by first indoctrinating them with an atheistic worldview.

The charge that Christians indoctrinate their children is an example of inconsistency, if not hypocrisy. The ACLU has successfully litigated God out of the public square and exiled Him from public schools. Public education from kindergarten to graduate school has strict regulations on free speech which, by their definition, does not include anything religious. The media has little control over its own biases, often failing to give Christianity a fair hearing.

Taking the new atheists at face value, one would think that Christians are really some kind of cult trying to control the world through myths and lies, murdering anyone who dares to stand in their way. While world domination is a frequent complaint, what about murder? Is that really part of the new atheists' criticisms of Christianity? Surprisingly, yes. In his introduction to *Letter to a Christian Nation*, Sam Harris says Christians are "murderously intolerant" of criticism. Richard Dawkins has stated in public lectures that the logical conclusion of monotheism is that anyone who opposes it must convert or die, regardless of the teaching of Christianity against such forced conversion.

The mass of anti-Christian propaganda put out by the new atheists is just that. Their work is conspicuously devoid of facts or logical arguments. They claim that Christianity is abusive, but include no descriptions of accompanying psychological problems associated with abuse evident among Christian children. They claim Christianity has murdered millions, but fail to cite numbers or locations of supposed mass executions. They claim that Christians are attempting to dominate by setting up a theocracy, yet offer little proof of that claim. In the end, they are just as allergic to facts as the Christians they claim to oppose.

Is Christianity Poisonous?

According to the new atheists, Christianity is Public Enemy Number One. All you have to do is pick up a copy of Dawkins's *The God Delusion,* Harris's *Letter to a Christian Nation,* or Hitchens's *God is Not Great: How Religion Poisons Everything* to see their indictment of the heinous religion known as *Christianity*. The last one is a real gem, because I don't know of any other book whose author sounds so utterly brilliant in his abject ignorance. It isn't that Hitchens is unintelligent—both he and Richard Dawkins were voted fifth and third in a list of the Top 100 public intellectuals in the world in 2005—he just seems all too eager to condemn a religion he fails to understand. That seems to be the trend with all of the new atheists.

The new atheists are quite fond of pointing out the supposed atrocities committed by Christians in the course of the last two millennia. They cite the Spanish Inquisition, the Crusades, and the Salem witch trials as evidence that Christianity is not only harmful but violent and dangerous. What these writers do not consider is that the supposed abuses of which Christians have been guilty for the last two thousand years stem not from genuine practice but perversion. It is the consistent failure to follow the teachings of Christ that led to the Spanish Inquisition and other terrible things such as the practice by medieval European monarchs of converting the infidel at the point of a sword.

What about all the good things Christianity has done? That thorny little problem gets sidestepped completely. For instance, critics fail to consider that Christianity is responsible for modern hospitals, whose names frequently derive from Christianity. While the modern healthcare industry has renamed many of them, we can still see the influence of Christianity in names like St. Jude's Children's Research Hospital in Memphis, Tennessee and St. Joseph's Hospital and Medical Center in Phoenix, Arizona.

We could turn to examine universities in the West. Virtually all of the Ivy League schools in the northeast retain their original mottos, which are drawn from the Bible or from Christian theology. Nearly all of these institutions began as schools to train ministers, and even as late as the 1800s many of them graduated as many ministers as students in all other fields of study combined. The university originally began in the medieval period as an outgrowth of monastic reform movements. In time they became stand-alone institutions that only recently have begun to neglect their original calling of preparing students for ministry.

Orphanages are another example of Christianity at work. The Mosaic Law, the same law that the new atheists claim has been used to callously and violently repress and oppress others for thousands of years, indicates that believers are to care for the less fortunate. The widow, the orphan, and the "stranger in the land" (resident alien) are singled out for help because it was easy to take advantage of such people in the ancient world, just as much as it is today. Orphanages were established to meet this need. All of them provided religious instruction for children, manned by those who served others out of love for God and obedience to His commands to care for the downtrodden and disempowered.

Surely You Can Do Better Than That

The literary contributions of the new atheists are vastly inferior to earlier critiques of faith offered by sober thinkers. Gone are the days of the existentialist philosophers Albert Camus and Jean-Paul

Sartre, as well as the nihilistic philosopher Friedrich Nietzsche. Part of the reason for the increased popularity of atheism was the literary skill of these three writers. Although all three were philosophers at heart, each one had a gift for communicating complex philosophical concepts in a popular and accessible manner. Camus wrote several novellas, one of the most famous of which is *The Outsider* (also translated as *The Stranger*). Sartre was a gifted playwright, famous for his play *No Exit*, but equally famous for his short book *Nausea* (in which he called man a "useless passion"). Even Nietzsche is engaging and does not read like dry, boring philosophy. His *The Parable of the Madman* is a classic expression of his belief in the death of God.

The new atheists are noticeably less talented than their unbelieving forebears. The "old" atheists differed a great deal from their newer counterparts, in part because they understood logic and knew how to make a good argument. Hitchens is probably the best writer among the new breed, but his work is full of factual mistakes. Richard Dawkins's *The God Delusion* has its share of errors, as well as a huge number of logical errors, ranging well into the dozens. Harris is just as error prone, adding a heavy dose of melodrama in his work. While these men and others like them are good communicators, one must observe both the form and substance of their messages. While they sound impressive, their merit is limited by the fact that basic mistakes are splattered across every other page.

The fact that the new atheists have become so popular is troublesome because people are no longer equipped with analytical skills. Logic is no longer taught in high schools, and modern education is consumed with testing to provide evidence of results. It is sad that learning has been replaced with testing, and that material aimed to encourage critical thinking seems to have gone into exile in favor of testable matter that students simply absorb through rote memorization. Thoughtful analysis is becoming increasingly rare.

This lack of critical thought has helped allow criticism of Christianity to gain such a foothold in the world today. TV documentaries boldly announce that they have uncovered "truth," which is really nothing more than a poor interpretation. Badly construed facts are fed to an audience composed largely of those who do not know how to evaluate them properly.

Anything But a Fool's Errand

Critics frequently caricature Christians as simple-minded and superstitious, fully intending to believe in a mythical God whose existence science has disproved. Consequently, it is allegedly the intellectual elite who believe in science and reason. Only the religious have IQs low enough to believe in God, goblins, and all manner of hocus-pocus.

A quick glance is all that is needed to discover that some of the most brilliant minds in human history placed their trust in the God of the Bible. Many of the great scientists were believers. Isaac Newton (mathematics), Blaise Paschal (mathematics, philosophy), Robert Boyle (chemistry), and Johannes Kepler (astronomy) all believed in God. Some would quickly point out, however, that these men all lived at times when atheism was intellectually disreputable. It simply wasn't fashionable to be an atheist so they chose to be religious rather than suffer the consequences. That argument is true, to an extent. It is one thing to pass oneself off as religious. It is quite another to profess an active belief in God as these men did, and many of them credited Him with their discoveries.

Let's say for a moment that we confine our search within the parameters of history since the Enlightenment, when religious belief in the West began its decline. But let's further restrict our search to thinkers in the last century. I doubt many would disagree with that, since Europe was mostly secular at that point and religious faith had dwindled to virtually nil. Now what do we have?

We could start with C.S. Lewis (1898-1963), whose intellect is unquestionable. He taught for years at Oxford University, one of the most prestigious institutions of higher learning in the world. He is known for penetrating insights and intellectual brilliance in articulating the truths of the Christian faith. What did Lewis have to say about his conversion to Christianity? Only that he was "the most dejected and reluctant convert in all England."

We could mention Alexander Solzhenitsyn (1918-2008), a Russian novelist and historian. Awarded the Nobel Prize in Literature in 1970, Solzhenitsyn made the world aware of the Soviet gulag, a system of penal labor camps in which millions died. He grew up under a regime that carefully indoctrinated its citizens against belief in God, yet he was a member of the Russian Orthodox Church.

Moving back into the sciences, we could mention prominent figures such as Francis Collins, handpicked by then President Bill Clinton to head the Human Genome Project, or Raymond Damadian, a young earth creationist who invented the MRI. Kurt Wise, a young earth creationist frequently mentioned by Richard Dawkins, obtained his Ph.D. in paleontology under Steven Jay Gould, one of the most prominent evolutionists of the twentieth century. John Lennox, professor of mathematics in the University of Oxford, is another prominent intellectual who has stood his ground against the likes of Dawkins and the new atheists. Alister McGrath, who has Ph.D.s in both microbiology and in theology from Oxford University, has also publicly defended the Christian faith.

By bringing up a list of famous believers, some opponents will cry foul. If we say, "Here's a list of really smart Christians, so Christianity must be true," then we would be guilty of a logical fallacy known as the fallacy of appeal to authority. We cannot say that something is true just because smart people believe it to be true. However, we aren't saying that Christianity is true because brilliant thinkers like Lewis, Solzhenitsyn, and others believe in God. We are simply saying that Christianity is an intelligent alternative to unbelief. That's the point. According to the new atheists, Christians are anti-science, anti-logic, and anti-reason. On the popular level, it is sometimes claimed that all believers are so; yet there are a vast number of God-fearing people who are scientifically minded, logical, and reasonable. This means that the idea that Christianity is an idiot's tale needs to be revised in light of the evidence. After all, the critics demand that we carefully examine the evidence, don't they?

Last Things Last

So what is one to do about the new atheism that seems to be sweeping the Western world? Even atheists condemn the extremism of the new atheism. For instance, Michael Ruse is quoted on the cover of Alister McGrath's *The Dawkins Delusion* as saying, "*The God Delusion* makes me embarrassed to be an atheist, and the McGraths show why." In a private email (later leaked) Ruse said to American philosopher Daniel Dennett:

> I think that you and Richard [Dawkins] are absolute disasters in the fight against intelligent design—we are losing this battle . . . what we need is not knee-jerk atheism but serious grappling with the issues—neither of you are willing to study Christianity seriously and to engage with the ideas—it is just plain silly and grotesquely immoral to claim that Christianity is simply a force for evil, as Richard claims—more than this, we are in a fight, and we need to make allies in the fight, not simply alienate everyone of good will.[iv]

The new strand of atheism has its fair share of critics, some of whom share its unbelief without its militant attitude.

On a final note, there are a few points to keep in mind:

The importance of the mind. Christians have a reputation—well-earned in some cases—of failing to use critical thinking skills. It's fairly common for critics to point out that Christians tell others to "just believe" and they will understand why God exists, while scientifically minded skeptics use hard evidence. This caricature of believers as empty-headed automatons is vastly overplayed, but, as Mark Twain once said, "The most outrageous lies that can be invented will find believers if a person only tells them with all his might." The new atheists are confident; it falls to Christians to be just as confident.

God doesn't want anyone to perish. If we approach the subject realizing that God does not delight in the destruction of the wicked, the conflict will take on a whole new meaning. The popular media is quite fond of showing the intolerance of believers, usually in the form of street preachers on public sidewalks screaming that everyone else is going to hell. It is of utmost importance to remember that presenting the truth in love will disarm many skeptics who perceive Christians as judgmental and intolerant.

Realize that it's not "us" against "them." Presenting the truth in love is an important piece of the puzzle. Jesus reached out to others that were considered social undesirables, such as the Syrophoenician woman (Mark 7:25-30) and the Samaritan woman at Jacob's well (John 4:1-42). We cannot forget the fact that Jesus asked His Father to forgive His murderers even in the midst of untold agony on the cross (Luke 23:34), and Stephen did the same while being bludgeoned to death in a hail of stones (Acts 7:54-59). Giving unbelievers a good reason to investigate Christian claims is one of the best things we can do. It isn't a matter of rebuking or lecturing someone who is inferior.

It is simply one pauper telling another where he found the greatest treasure in the world.

Study Guide

In the study guide for this book, we're going to ask some tough questions. Peter tells Christians that we need to be prepared to answer questions when they arise (1 Peter 3:15). If we're doing our jobs as salt and light in the world around us (Matthew 5:13-16), then we're going to be questioned.

Truth 1: We Can Know Truth

Think It Through
1. Why is it that some people misunderstand the Bible?
2. How many different ways is truth defined in our culture today?
3. What is the importance of proper thinking?

How It Makes a Difference
1. What place does reason and logic have in your faith?
2. How can you continue to increase using your mind in reading the Bible?

When Someone Asks
1. "You've got your truth, and I've got my truth. Why should I change?"
2. "Isn't having just one kind of truth a bit narrow-minded?"
3. "How can you say that relativism isn't true when so many people disagree?"

The Best Defense
1. How would you respond to a fellow Christian who argues that faith does not need any evidence?
2. Using both logic and the Bible, how do you respond to the claim that "all truth is relative"?
3. In what ways can the relativist be exclusive?

Truth 2: The Universe Had a Creator

Think It Through
1. What or who could have made the universe, other than God?
2. Observation is a key component to the scientific method. Why is this a problem for the Big Bang theory?

How It Makes a Difference
1. Compared to the vast size of the universe, our solar system is just a speck of dust. Yet God gives man a great deal of attention in the Bible. What does this say about God? What does it say about man?
2. As part of God's creation, what does that say about our responsibilities to Him?

When Someone Asks
1. "I agree with Carl Sagan when he says the universe has been here forever. Why shouldn't I?"

2. "Haven't scientists already decided that the Big Bang is the cause of the universe?"

The Best Defense
1. Give an explanation why the universe must have had an adequate cause for it to exist.
2. Give a detailed reason why the Big Bang is an inadequate explanation for the universe's origin. Include a discussion of the Oscillating Universe model.

Truth 3: God Exists

Think It Through
1. What does the apparent design of the universe have to say about God?
2. Why does God have authority?

How It Makes a Difference
1. In what way does having certainty about God's existence impact your faith?
2. What are the pros and cons of the argument from religious experience?

When Someone Asks
1. "Isn't Christianity a cop-out for people too weak to handle the real world?"
2. "Hasn't science disproved religion?"

The Best Defense
1. Outline what you think is the best argument for the existence of God.
2. Put yourself in the shoes of a non-Christian. Do you think your argument holds up, or do you need to fine-tune it? How?

Truth 4: The Bible Is Historically Reliable

Think It Through
1. What should be the Christian's approach to history?
2. How is the Bible portrayed in the media?

How It Makes a Difference
1. Of all the religions from the ancient world, only the Judeo-Christian worldview connects itself to reality. What does this say to you?
2. What evidence from history gives you the greatest confidence about the Bible's claims regarding Jesus?

When Someone Asks
1. "The Bible is just a book of myths like any other, right?"
2. "There are many intelligent people who question the Bible. Why don't you trust them?"

The Best Defense
1. How would you outline the best way of determining the trustworthiness of an ancient book?
2. Read the Gospels from the beginning of Matthew to the end of John. What are all the evidences of eyewitness testimony that you see?
3. The Bible includes embarrassing details about some of its most prominent characters. What do you think this says about the reliability of Scripture?

Truth 5: Archaeology Confirms the Bible's Reliability

Think It Through
1. What can archaeology prove?

Study Guide

2. Why can't archaeology directly prove the inspiration of the Bible?
3. A common charge is that the Bible has been corrupted through centuries of copying and cannot be trusted. What does archaeology say about this?

How It Makes a Difference
1. Archaeology can prove quite a bit about the Bible. What does this say to your faith?
2. What discoveries give you the greatest confidence in the trustworthiness of Scripture?

When Someone Asks
1. "Can you give me proof that the Old Testament is true?"
2. "I think the New Testament authors wrote great fiction, not truth. Why do you think the events of the Bible are true?"
3. "Why am I supposed to trust the Gospels?"

The Best Defense
1. List what you think are the three most compelling reasons why the Bible cannot be treated as a book of fairy tales.
2. Make a case for the importance of secular confirmation of biblical events.

Truth 6: Jesus Really Lived

Think It Through
1. What kind of credibility do the non-Christian mentions of Jesus lend to the Gospels?
2. In your opinion, what is the most convincing piece of evidence for the historicity of Jesus?
3. Why are hostile witnesses important?

How It Makes a Difference
1. What traits of Jesus do you admire most?
2. If Jesus really lived, then His life serves as an example for us to follow (1 Peter 2:21). What changes do you need to make in your life to be more Christlike?

When Someone Asks
1. "I've heard reasons why Jesus is just a myth. Why do you think Jesus was real?"
2. "Aren't the passages that refer to Jesus in Josephus just fabrications?"

The Best Defense
1. Write down the four most important reasons why Jesus was a real person. Explain why you chose these four points.
2. Explain why the Gospels are reliable sources for the life of Christ.
3. Identify four extrabiblical sources that mention Jesus and why they are important.

Truth 7: Jesus Was Raised from the Dead

Think It Through
1. What is some of the eyewitness testimony concerning the resurrection cited in the New Testament?
2. What is the biggest problem for those who don't believe in the resurrection?
3. How could the Jewish leaders have disproved the resurrection if it were really a hoax?

How It Makes a Difference
1. What does the resurrection of Jesus mean to you?

2. If Jesus was raised from the dead, what does that say about your eternal future?

When Someone Asks
1. "How do you know Jesus was raised from the dead?"
2. "Wasn't Jesus just like any other religious leader or spiritual guru?"

The Best Defense
1. List the ways modern people try to explain away the resurrection of Christ. Based on what we covered in this and the previous three chapters, what are the problems with each explanation?
2. Give a list of details concerning the resurrection of Christ that meet the criteria for the "principle of embarrassment."
3. Read 1 Corinthians 15:1-11 closely. What details stand out in this passage, and why do they deserve serious consideration?

Truth 8: Pain and Suffering Do Not Disprove God's Existence

Think It Through
1. What does the Bible say about the ultimate end of pain and suffering?
2. In what ways does the Bible's teaching try to minimize evil, pain, and suffering?
3. Why is it inconsistent for a relativist to talk about the problem of evil?
4. In what ways can pain be beneficial?

How It Makes a Difference
1. Though mankind enjoys freedom of choice, it also means that some will abuse that freedom. What does this say about the responsibility we have to God?

2. Does knowing that your sin contributes to the pain of others make you want to live a more perfect life? Why?

When Someone Asks
1. "How can God let people get away with murder, rape, and other crimes without consequence?"
2. "Why does God let people suffer? Why doesn't He stop all evil right now?"
3. "Why do you think Freud was wrong when he argued that man invented religion to empower himself?"

The Best Defense
1. Outline your response to the problem of evil, pain, and suffering and the existence of God.
2. What is a good argument for God's existence in the face of personal tragedy?
3. Although many ask why so much evil exists, an equally valid question is why *more* evil doesn't exist. How would you frame an argument for God's existence based on the good we see around us?

Truth 9: The Bible Is Inspired

Think It Through
1. How is the Bible different from other works of literature in the ancient world?
2. What reasons might a person have for wanting to find contradictions in the Bible?

How It Makes a Difference
1. What does it mean to have the Word of God rather than mythical or fictional literature as a holy book?

2. What does it mean to you to have a book that has been crafted by God Himself?

When Someone Asks
1. "How do you know the Bible came from God?"
2. "How do you know that the Bible wasn't just cobbled together from different writers?"

The Best Defense
1. Make a cogent argument for the inspiration of the Bible. What realistic qualities or characteristics would you expect from an inspired book, and what would you expect from an uninspired book?
2. Other people in history have claimed to be prophets for God or other religions. What differences do you see in the nature of their claims versus the types of claims made by the authors of Scripture?

Truth 10: Christianity Is Unique

Think It Through
1. Why do some people claim the Bible is nothing more than ancient mythology?
2. In what ways is Jesus different from other great teachers in history?
3. What are the reasons for claiming that Jesus is unique?

How It Makes a Difference
1. What does it mean to you knowing that Christianity makes unique claims?
2. What are the implications of this uniqueness?

When Someone Asks
1. "Why do you think Christianity is different from any other world religion?"

2. "Don't you think it's arrogant to claim that Christianity is unique—and therefore better—than other religions?"

The Best Defense
1. In what ways is Christianity unique from other religions, and how do you explain any similarities between them?
2. List the different ways Jesus is interpreted and give a rebuttal for each point.

Truth 11: Early Christians Were Not Plagiarists

Think It Through
1. What are some problems early Christians would have faced if they had plagiarized other religions?
2. What differences do you see in the character of God and Jesus in comparison to the Greek gods?

How It Makes a Difference
1. What does it mean to you knowing that Jesus can be securely located in history?
2. Why is it inadequate to think of Jesus as nothing more than a teacher of good morals, a philosopher, or a first-century rabbi?

When Someone Asks
1. "Why should you think of the Bible as historical and not mythological?"
2. "Isn't the story of Jesus just a myth borrowed from other religions?"

The Best Defense
1. Someone asks you about a movie they've seen lately that says the early Christians ripped off various pagan religions. What do you say?

2. Define myth, legend, and fairy tale. What differences do you see between each one and the Bible?

Truth 12: God Loves Sinners

Think It Through
1. What is sin, and why is it so serious?
2. Can a loving God also be a just God? How?
3. How does the Bible define love?
4. How is the universal love of God demonstrated in the life of Christ?

How It Makes a Difference
1. Does knowing that we have salvation only through Christ's sacrifice change how you live your life?
2. God created the world knowing that He would have to send His son to redeem it. What does this say about God?
3. What does Romans 3:9-20 say about those who don't think they're all that bad?
4. How is the biblical idea of sin twisted in modern culture?

When Someone Asks
1. "I've done terrible things in my life that I can't forgive myself for. Why should God forgive me?"
2. "Why would Jesus give His life for me?"

The Best Defense
1. Make a list of all the ways that God shows love to His people in the Bible.
2. How would you argue for the final justification of good and evil without making it sound like Christianity is just waiting for the "pie in the sky"?

Appendix: New Atheism Isn't New

Think It Through
1. How does modern culture portray Christianity?
2. What are the different kinds of unbelief that you can think of?
3. In your opinion, what would make a person want to not believe in God?

How It Makes a Difference
1. Can Christians have an intelligent faith?
2. Considering the intellectual problems of the new atheism, would this impact how you would talk about your faith?
3. Because atheism is becoming increasingly popular, how does this affect your hope that others will believe in God?

When Someone Asks
1. "What is the difference between martyrs in the early church and suicide bombers who are also considered martyrs?"
2. "I recently read a book written by a famous atheist and I don't know what to think about my faith now. Do you think there is something to this stuff?"
3. "These new atheists all have high-powered degrees from prestigious schools. Doesn't that mean I should consider what they have to say?"

The Best Defense
1. Contrast modern arguments against the ancient writers of Scripture. What are some of the unrealistic expectations of the Bible?
2. What problems do you see in the hostile approach against Christianity taken by the new atheists?
3. Outline your response to the charge that religion is harmful.

Endnotes

Truth 1 notes
i   Paul Copan, *True for You but Not for Me: Deflating the Slogans that Leave Christians Speechless* (Minneapolis: Bethany House, 1998), 83.

ii   Amy Orr-Ewing, *Is Believing in God Irrational?* (Downers Grove: InterVarsity Press, 2008), 62.

iii   Allan Bloom, *The Closing of the American Mind* (New York: Simon & Schuster, 1987), 25.

Truth 2 notes
i   R.C. Sproul, *Not a Chance* (Grand Rapids: Baker Books, 1994), 6.

ii   Carl Sagan, *Cosmos* (New York: Random House, 1980), 4.

iii   Brad Lemley, "Why is There Life?" *Discover* (November 2000), http://discovermagazine.com/2000/nov/cover/?searchterm=Brad%20lemley%20why%20is%20there%20life

iv   Ibid.

v   Andrew Snelling, "Radioactive 'dating' failure: Recent New Zealand lava flows yield 'ages' of millions of years." December 1, 1999, http://www.answersingenesis.org/articles/cm/v22/n1/dating#r7

vi Steven Austin, "Excess argon within mineral concentrates from the new dacite lava dome at Mount St Helens volcano," December 1996. http://www.answersingenesis.org/tj/v10/i3/argon.asp

vii Hillary Mayell, "T. Rex Soft Tissue Found Preserved," March 24, 2005. http://news.nationalgeographic.com/news/2005/03/0324_050324_trexsofttissue.html

viii Scott Norris, "Many Dino Fossils Could Have Soft Tissue Inside," February 22, 2006. http://news.nationalgeographic.com/news/2006/02/0221_060221_dino_tissue.html

Truth 3 notes

i John Leo, "At Postmodern U., professors who see no evil," *Jewish World Review*, 16 July 2002, www.jewishworldreview.com/cols/leo071602.asp.

ii Bertrand Russell, *Autobiography*, Vol. 3 (New York: Simon and Schuster, 1969), 29.

iii Rick Weiss, "Prize Fight: Raymond Damadian refuses to take his failure to win a Nobel Prize, for a prototype MRI machine, lying down," *Smithsonian* magazine, December 2003, http://www.smithsonianmag.com/science-nature/Prize_Fight.html.

Truth 4 notes

i www.gallup.com/poll/22885/twentyeight-percent-believe-bible-actual-word-god.aspx.

ii William Ramsay, *St. Paul the Traveler and the Roman Citizen* (Grand Rapids: Baker Books, 1982), 8.

Truth 5 notes

i Nelson Glueck, *Rivers in the Desert: History of Negev* (Philadelphia: Jewish Publication Society of America, 1969), 31.

ii William. M. Ramsay, *The Bearing of Recent Discovery on the Trustworthiness of the New Testament,* 4th ed. (London: Hodder and Stoughton, 1920), 222.

iii William Foxwell Albright, *The Archaeology and Religion of Israel*, 1st ed. (Baltimore, MD: The Johns Hopkins Press, 1943), 176.

Truth 6 notes

i Eric J. Lyman, "Italian atheist sues priest over Jesus' existence," Jan. 30, 2006, http://www.usatoday.com/news/religion/2006-01-30-italy-atheist_x.htm.

"Did Jesus exist? Case dismissed, CNN.com, Feb. 10, 2006, http://www.religionnewsblog.com/13597.

Joe Kovacs, worldnetdaily.com, "Atheist who sued priest over Jesus' reality fined," July 3, 2006, http://www.religionnewsblog.com/15169/atheist-who-sued-priest-over-Jesus-reality-fined

ii Simon Greenleaf, *The Testimony of the Evangelists: Examined by the Rules of Evidence Administered in Courts of Justice* (Grand Rapids, MI: Baker Book House, 1874, 1965), 2.

iii Tacitus, Annals 15.44

iv Gary Habermas, *The Historical Jesus*, 190.

v Suetonius, Claudius, 25. There is genuine debate over whether the name Chrestus, which was a common one at the time, refers to a man living in Rome or to Christ. Since the spelling is virtually identical to that used by Tacitus, many scholars nevertheless conclude that Suetonius' reference does indeed point to Christ.

vi Pliny the Younger, Letters, 10.96.

vii Josephus, Antiquities, 20:9.

viii Josephus, Antiquities, 18:3.

ix H. Wayne House, *The Jesus Who Never Lived: Exposing False Christs and Finding the Real Jesus* (Eugene, OR: Harvest House, 2008), 61.

x Charlesworth, *Jesus Within Judaism*, 24, cited in Habermas, *The Historical Jesus*, 195.

xi Habermas, 203.

xii David Mills, *Atheist Universe: The Thinking Person's Answer to Christian Fundamentalism* (Berkeley, CA: Ulysses Press, 2006), 36.

xiii Will Durant, *The Story of Civilization, vol. 3: Caesar and Christ* (New York: Simon & Schuster: 1944), 557.

Truth 7 Notes
i   Philo of Alexandria, *In Flaccum*, 83-85
ii   Michael F. Bird and James G. Crossley, *How Did Christianity Begin? A Believer and Non-Believer Examine the Evidence* (Peabody, MA: Hendrickson Publishers, Inc., 2008), 49.
iii   Lucian of Samosata, *The Death of Peregrine*, 11-12. (Works of Lucian of Samosata, vol 4.)

Truth 8 notes
i   The OmniPoll, conducted by Barna Research Group, Ltd., January, 1999, http://www.equip.org/articles/why-does-god-allow-suffering-
ii   Lee Strobel, *The Case for Faith* (Grand Rapids: Zondervan Publishing House, 2000), 14.
iii   C.S. Lewis, *Mere Christianity* (New York: HarperCollins, 1980), 48.
iv   Bart D. Ehrman, *God's Problem: How the Bible Fails to Answer Our Most Important Question—Why We Suffer* (New York: HarperOne, 2008), 6-19.
v   David Hume, *Dialogues Concerning Natural Religion*, ed. Norman Kemp Smith (New York: Thomas Nelson & Sons, 1947; Library of Liberal Arts, 1979), 196.

Truth 10 notes
i   R. C. Sproul, *Reason to Believe*, 38.
ii   Origen, *Homily on Luke 1:11*, quoted in Wilhelm Schneemelcher, ed., *New Testament Apocrypha*, trans. R. McL. Wilson, vol 1 of *Gospels and Related Writings* (Louisville: John Knox Press, 1991), 46.

Truth 11 notes
i   Timothy Freke and Peter Gandy, *The Jesus Mysteries:* (New York: Three Rivers, 1999), 9.

Endnotes

ii Tom Harpur, *The Pagan Christ* (New York: Walker & Company, 2004), 10.

iii J. Ed Komoszewski, M. James Sawyer, and Daniel B. Wallace, *Reinventing Jesus: What the Da Vinci Code and Other Novel Speculations Don't Tell You* (Grand Rapids: Kregel Publications, 2006), 222.

iv Bruce Metzger, ed. *Historical and Literary Studies: Pagan, Jewish, and Christian*, New Testament Tools and Studies 8 (Grand Rapids: Eerdmans, 1968), 9.

Truth 13 notes

i Richard Dawkins, "Religion's Real Child Abuse," *Free Inquiry*, 22.4 (Fall 2002), 12.

ii Christopher Hitchens, *God is Not Great*, 217.

iii http://www.wired.com/wired/archive/14.11/atheism.html?pg=2&topic=atheism&topic_set=

iv Michael Ruse, personal email to Daniel Dennett, Feb. 19, 2006, http://www.uncommondescent.com/intelligent-design/the-ruse-dennett-briefwechsel-the-clash-between-evolution-and-evolutionism/

Bibliography

Albright, William Foxwell. *The Archaeology and Religion of Israel*, 1st ed. Baltimore, MD: The Johns Hopkins Press, 1943.

Austin, Steven "Excess argon within mineral concentrates from the new dacite lava dome at Mount St Helens volcano," December 1996. http://www.answersingenesis.org/tj/v10/i3/argon.asp

Bird Michael F. and James G. Crossley, *How Did Christianity Begin? A Believer and Non-Believer Examine the Evidence*. Peabody, MA: Hendrickson Publishers, Inc., 2008.

Bloom, Allan. *The Closing of the American Mind*. New York, NY: Simon & Schuster, 1987.

Copan, Paul. *True for You but Not for Me: Deflating the Slogans that Leave Christians Speechless*. Minneapolis, MN: Bethany House, 1998.

Dawkins, Richard. "Religion's Real Child Abuse," *Free Inquiry*, 22.4 (Fall 2002).

Durant, Will. *The Story of Civilization, vol. 3: Caesar and Christ*. New York: Simon & Schuster: 1944.

Ehrman, Bart D. *God's Problem: How the Bible Fails to Answer Our Most Important Question—Why We Suffer*. New York: HarperOne, 2008.

Freke, Timothy and Peter Gandy. *The Jesus Mysteries: Was the "Original Jesus" a Pagan God?* New York: Three Rivers, 1999.

Glueck, Nelson. *Rivers in the Desert: History of Negev.* Philadelphia, PA: Jewish Publication Society of America, 1969.

Greenleaf, Simon. *The Testimony of the Evangelists: Examined by the Rules of Evidence Administered in Courts of Justice.* Grand Rapids, MI: Baker Book House, 1965.

Habermas, Gary. *The Historical Jesus: Ancient Evidence for the Life of Christ.* Joplin, MO: College Press, 1996.

Harpur, Tom *The Pagan Christ: Recovering the Lost Light.* New York: Walker & Company, 2004.

Hitchens, Christopher. *God is Not Great: How Religion Poisons Everything.* New York: Twelve Books, 2007.

House, H. Wayne. *The Jesus Who Never Lived: Exposing False Christs and Finding the Real Jesus.* Eugene, OR: Harvest House, 2008.

Hume, David. *Dialogues Concerning Natural Religion*, ed. Norman Kemp Smith. New York: Thomas Nelson & Sons, 1947.

Komoszewski, J. Ed, M. James Sawyer, and Daniel B. Wallace, *Reinventing Jesus: What the Da Vinci Code and Other Novel Speculations Don't Tell You.* Grand Rapids, MI: Kregel Publications, 2006.

Kovacs, Joe. worldnetdaily.com, "Atheist who sued priest over Jesus' reality fined," July 3, 2006. http://www.religionnewsblog.com/15169/atheist-who-sued-priest-over-Jesus-reality-fined

Lemley, Brad. "Why is There Life?" Discover (November 2000). http://discovermagazine.com/2000/nov/cover/?searchterm=Brad%20lemley%20why%20is%20there%20life

Leo, John. "At Postmodern U., professors who see no evil," *Jewish World Review*, 16 July 2002. www.jewishworldreview.com/cols/leo071602.asp.

Lewis, C.S. *Mere Christianity.* New York: HarperCollins, 1980.

Lyman, Eric J. "Italian atheist sues priest over Jesus' existence," Jan. 30, 2006. http://www.usatoday.com/news/religion/2006-01-30-italy-atheist_x.htm.

Mayell, Hillary. "T. Rex Soft Tissue Found Preserved," March 24, 2005. http://news.nationalgeographic.com/news/2005/03/0324_050324_trexsofttissue.html

Metzger, Bruce, ed. *Historical and Literary Studies: Pagan, Jewish, and Christian, New Testament Tools and Studies 8.* Grand Rapids, MI: Eerdmans, 1968.

Mills, David. *Atheist Universe: The Thinking Person's Answer to Christian Fundamentalism.* Berkeley, CA: Ulysses Press, 2006.

Newport, Frank. "Twenty-Eight Percent Believe Bible is Actual Word of God." May 22, 2006. www.gallup.com/poll/22885/twentyeight-percent-believe-bible-actual-word-god.aspx

Norris, Scott. "Many Dino Fossils Could Have Soft Tissue Inside," February 22, 2006. http://news.nationalgeographic.com/news/2006/02/0221_060221_dino_tissue.html

Orr-Ewing, Amy. *Is Believing in God Irrational?* Downers Grove, IL: InterVarsity Press, 2008.

Ramsay, William M. *The Bearing of Recent Discovery on the Trustworthiness of the New Testament, 4th ed.* London: Hodder and Stoughton, 1920.

_____. *St. Paul the Traveler and the Roman Citizen.* Grand Rapids: Baker Books 1982.

Russell, Bertrand. *Autobiography, Vol. 3.* New York, NY: Simon and Schuster, 1969.

Sagan, Carl. *Cosmos.* New York, NY: Random House, 1980.

Schneemelcher, Wilhelm, ed., *New Testament Apocrypha, trans. R. McL. Wilson, vol 1 of Gospels and Related Writings.* Louisville, KY: John Knox Press, 1991.

Snelling, Andrew. "Radioactive 'dating' failure: Recent New Zealand lava flows yield 'ages' of millions of years." December 1, 1999. http://www.answersingenesis.org/articles/cm/v22/n1/dating#r7

Sproul, R.C. *Not a Chance.* Grand Rapids, MI: Baker Books, 1994.

_____. *Reason to Believe: A Response to Common Objections to Christianity.* Grand Rapids, MI Zondervan, 1982.

Strobel, Lee. *The Case for Faith*. Grand Rapids, MI: Zondervan, 2000.

Weiss, Rick. "Prize Fight: Raymond Damadian refuses to take his failure to win a Nobel Prize, for a prototype MRI machine, lying down," *Smithsonian* magazine, December 2003. http://www.smithsonianmag.com/science-nature/Prize_Fight.html.

www.ingramcontent.com/pod-product-compliance
Lightning Source LLC
LaVergne TN
LVHW051600070426
835507LV00021B/2681